Gypsy Witch Book of Old Pennsylvania Dutch Pow-Wows and Hexes

Includes *Pow-Wows, Or, The Long Lost Friend*

&

King Zoltan's The Mystic Oracle - Based on Systems of the Ancients

With Additional Material By Dragonstar and Tim R. Swartz

INNER LIGHT PUBLICATIONS

Gypsy Witch Book of Old Pennsylvania Dutch Pow-Wows and Hexes

GYPSY WITCH BOOK OF OLD PENNSYLVANIA DUTCH POW-WOWS AND HEXES

Additional Material by Dragonstar and Tim R. Swartz

Copyright © 2009 - Inner Light Publications, All Rights Reserved

ISBN-10: 1606110721
ISBN-13: 9781606110720

Nonfiction – Metaphysics

No part of this book may be reproduced, stored in retrieval system or transmitted in any form or by any means, electronic, mechanical, photocopying, recording, without express permission of the publisher.

Timothy Green Beckley: Editorial Director
Carol Rodriguez: Publishers Assistant
Tim Swartz: Associate Editor
Sean Casteel: Editorial Assistant
William Kern: Editorial Assistant
Cover Art: Tim Swartz

1. Beckley, Timothy, Dragonstar, Swartz, Tim, Magical Arts, Metaphysics, History – Nonfiction
I. Title: Gypsy Witch Book of Old Pennsylvania Dutch Pow-Wows and Hexes

133'.4

For free catalog write:
Global Communications
P.O. Box 753
New Brunswick, NJ 08903

Free Subscription to Conspiracy Journal E-Mail Newsletter
www.conspiracyjournal.com

Gypsy Witch Book of Old Pennsylvania Dutch Pow-Wows and Hexes

Contents

THE HIDDEN ROOTS OF POW-WOW
By Dragonstar

-4-

POW-WOW, OR, THE LONG LOST FRIEND
By John George Hohman

-6-

**FORBIDDEN SECRETS OF MYSTICAL KNOWLEDGE—
FOR ONLY A DIME**
By Tim R. Swartz

-90-

**KING ZOLTAN'S MYSTIC ORACLE –
BASED ON SYSTEMS OF THE ANCIENTS**
By King Zoltan

-93-

Gypsy Witch Book of Old Pennsylvania Dutch Pow-Wows and Hexes

THE HIDDEN ROOTS OF POW-WOW
By Dragonstar

In 1820, John George Hohman published a book called *Verborgne Freund* (*Long Lost Friend*). In this book are ancient household remedies, incantations, and charms that are based on the magical practices of emigrants from the Rhineland and Switzerland who arrived in Pennsylvania in the 17th and 18th centuries. Powwowing (called by the Pennsylvania Dutch "braucha"), was primarily used for faith healing, but also employed various charms and incantations for protection against personal harm, thieves and hexes by witches and other evil people.

The term Pow-Wow was possibly derived from the early settlers' observations of the Algonquin Indian's Pow-Wows and merely adapted a popular term to a long-established custom. The word may also be a derivative of the word "power."

In a time when doctors were few and far between, people had to rely upon themselves in dealing with sickness and injuries. Faith healing and herbal cures were very popular, but were often frowned upon, if not outright banned by the Protestant Churches, who were attempting to separate "religion" from "superstition."

Even though powwowing was outlawed by the Protestant church, practioners attributes its power to the Christian God. Powwowers claim to be participants of God's healing power, middle-men through which God cures the faithful. The charms which the powwowers use, if not directly from the Bible, contain Christian references particularly to Jesus or Mary. The patient must be willing to repeat the Lord's Prayer and Apostle's Creed. Each charm concludes with "the three highest names" of Father, Son, and Holy Ghost (+ + +).

Powwowing was especially used to stop bleeding and to ease the pain of burns, sprains, cuts, and bruises. These charms were used not only on people, but also for farm animals whose good health was extremely important for rural farmers depended daily upon their horses and cattle.

Today, magic is generally condemned by most major religions and most so-called "good Christians" would be horrified to know that many common Christian rituals would be considered magic by their overly broad definitions. Powwowing uses these centuries-old Jewish and Christian magical traditions, handed down from generation to generation, a testament to faith in God in this age of science and technology.

Gypsy Witch Book of Old Pennsylvania Dutch Pow-Wows and Hexes

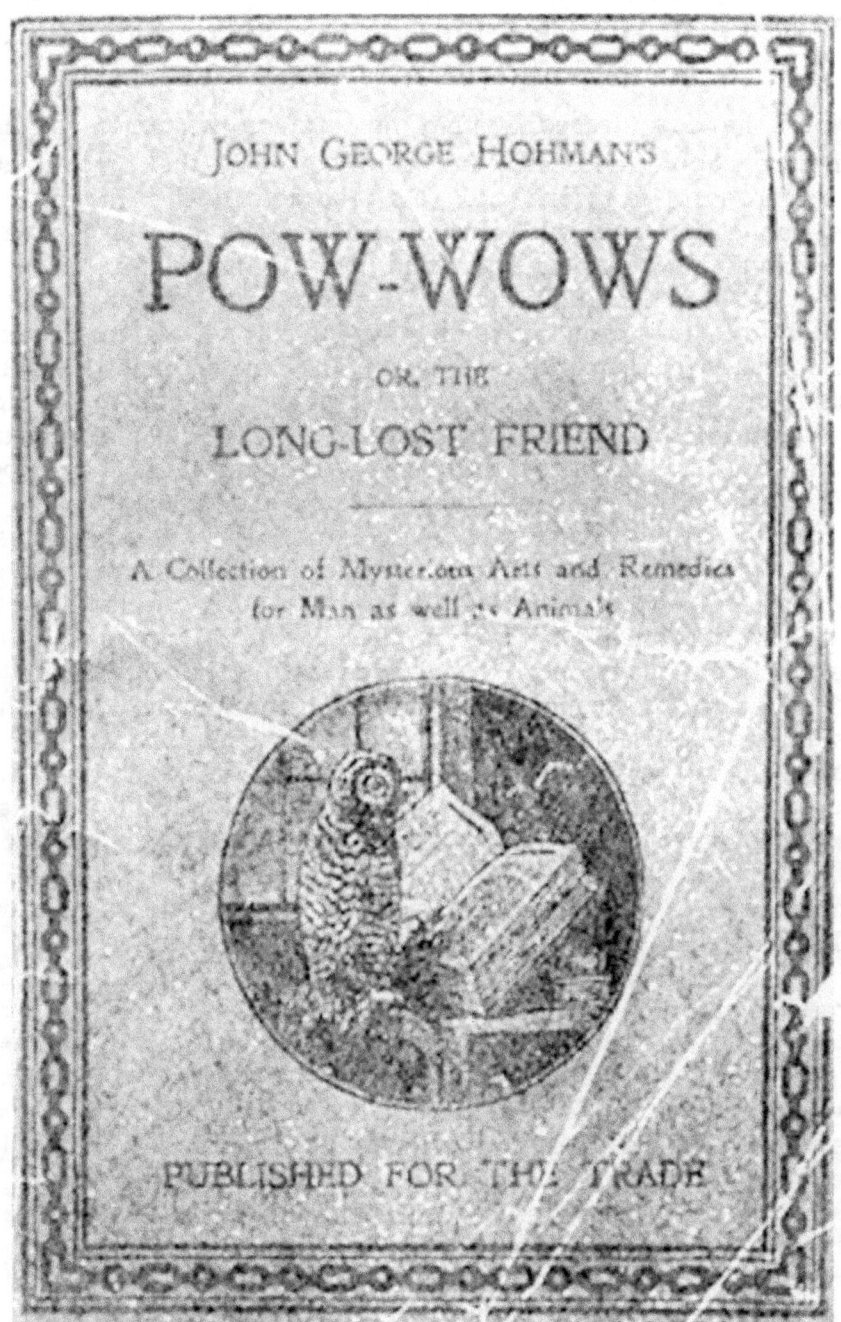

POW-WOWS; OR, THE LONG LOST FRIEND

Gypsy Witch Book of Old Pennsylvania Dutch Pow-Wows and Hexes

PREFACE TO THE FIRST EDITION OF THIS USEFUL BOOK

The author would have preferred writing no preface whatever to this little book, were it not indispensably necessary, in order to meet the erroneous views some men entertain in regard to works of this character. The majority, undoubtedly, approve of the publication and sale of such books, yet some are always found who will persist in denouncing them as something wrong. This latter class I cannot help but pity, for being so far led astray; and I earnestly pray everyone who might find it in his power, to bring them from off their ways of error. It is true, whosoever taketh the name of JESUS in vain, committeth a great sin. Yet, is it not expressly written in the fiftieth Psalm, according to Luther's translation: "Call upon me in the day of trouble; I will deliver thee, and thou shalt glorify me." In the Catholic translation, the same passage is found in the forty-ninth Psalm, reading thus: "Call upon me in the day of thy trouble, and I will deliver thee, and thou shalt glorify me."

Where is the doctor who has ever cured or banished the panting or palpitation of the heart, and hide-boundness? Where is the doctor who ever banished a wheal? Where is the doctor who ever banished the mother-fits? Where is the doctor that can cure mortification when it once seizes a member of the body? All these cures, and a great many more mysterious and wonderful things are contained in this book; and its author could take an oath at any time upon the fact of his having successfully applied many of the prescriptions contained herein.

I say: any and every man who knowingly neglects using this book in saving the eye, or the leg, or any other limb of his fellow-man, is guilty of the loss of such limb, and thus commits a sin, by which he may forfeit to himself all hope of salvation. Such men refuse to call upon the Lord in their trouble, although He especially commands it. If men were not allowed to use sympathetic words, nor the name of the MOST HIGH, it certainly would not have been revealed to them; and what is more, the Lord would not help where they are made use of. God can in no manner be forced to intercede where it is not his divine pleasure.

Another thing I have to notice here: There are men who will say, if one has used sympathetic words in vain, the medicines of doctors could not avail any, because the words did not effect a cure. This is only the excuse of physicians; because whatever cannot be cured by sympathetic words, can much less be cured by any doctor's craft or cunning. I could name at any time that Catholic priest whose horse was cured with mere words; and I could also give the name of the man who did it. I knew the priest well; he formerly resided in Westmoreland County. If it was desired, I could also name a Reformed preacher who cured several persons of the fever, merely by writing them some tickets for that purpose; and even the names of those persons I could mention. This preacher formerly resided in Berks County.

If men but use out of this book what they actually need, they surely commit no sin; yet woe unto those who are guilty that anyone loses his life in consequence of mortification, or loses a limb, or the sight of the eye! Woe unto those who misconstrue these things at the moment of danger, or who follow the ill advice of

Gypsy Witch Book of Old Pennsylvania Dutch Pow-Wows and Hexes

any preacher who might teach them not to mind what the Lord says in the fiftieth Psalm. "Call upon me in the day of trouble: I will deliver thee, and thou shalt glorify me." Woe unto those who, in obeying the directions of a preacher, neglect using any means offered by this book against mortification, or inflammation, or the wheal. I am willing to follow the preacher in all reasonable things, yet when I am in danger and he advises me not to use any prescriptions found in this book, in such a case I shall not obey him. And woe also unto those who use the name of the Lord in vain and for trifling purposes.

I have given many proofs of the usefulness of this book, and I could yet do it at any time. I sell my books publicly, and not secretly, as other mystical books are sold. I am willing that my books should be seen by everybody, and I shall not secrete or hide myself from any preacher. I, Hohman, too, have some knowledge of the Scriptures, and I know when to pray and call unto the Lord for assistance. The publication of books (provided they are useful and morally right) is not prohibited in the United States, as is the case in other countries where kings and despots hold tyrannical sway over the people. I place myself upon the broad platform of the liberty of the press and of conscience, in regard to this useful book, and it shall ever be my most heartfelt desire that all men might have an opportunity of using it to their good, in the name of Jesus.

Given at Rosenthal, near Reading, Berks county Penn., on the 31st day of July, in the year of our Lord, 1819.

JOHN GEORGE HOHMAN
Author and original publisher of this book

Gypsy Witch Book of Old Pennsylvania Dutch Pow-Wows and Hexes

TESTIMONIALS

Which go to show at any time, that I, Hohman, have successfully applied the prescriptions of this book.

BENJAMIN STOUDY, the son of a Lutheran schoolmaster, at Reading, suffered dreadfully from a wheal in the eye. In a little more than 24 hours, this eye was so sound as the other one, by the aid I rendered him with the help of God, in the year 1817.

HENRY JORGES, residing in Reading, brought to me a boy who suffered extreme pain, caused by a wheal in the eye, in the year 1814. In a little more than 24 hours, I, with the help of God, have healed him.

JOHN BAYER, son of Jacob Bayer, now living near Reading, had an ulcer on his leg, which gave him great pain. I attended him, and in a short time the leg was well. This was in the year 1818.

LANDLIN GOTTWALD, formerly residing in Reading, had a severe pain in his one arm. In about 24 hours I cured his arm.

CATHERINE MECK, at that time in Alsace Township, suffered very much from a wheal in the eye. In a little more that 24 hours the eye was healed.

MR. SILVIS, of Reading, came to my house while engaged at the brewery of my neighbor. He felt great pain in the eye caused by a wheal. I cured his eye in a little more than 24 hours.

ANNA SNYDER, of Alsace Township, had a severe pain in one of her fingers. In a little more than twenty-four hours she felt relieved.

MICHAEL HARTMAN, Jr., living in Alsace Township, had a child with a very sore mouth. I attended it and in a little more than twenty-four hours it was well again.

JOHN BINGEMANN, at Ruscombmanor, Berks County, had a boy who burnt himself dreadfully. My wife came to that place in the fall of the year 1812. Mortification has already set in — my wife had sympathy for it, and in a short time the mortification was banished. The boy was soon after perfectly cured and became well again. It was about the same time that my wife cured John Bingemann's wife of the wild-fire, which she had on a sore leg.

Gypsy Witch Book of Old Pennsylvania Dutch Pow-Wows and Hexes

SUSANNA GOMBER had a severe pain in the head. In a short time I relieved her.

The wife of David Brecht also felt a severe pain in the head, and was relieved by me in a short time.

JOHN JUNKINS' daughter and daughter-in-law both suffered very much from pain in the head; and his wife too had a sore cheek, on which the wild-fire had broken out severely. The headache of the daughter and the daughter-in-law was banished by me; and the wild-fire of the wife was cured in some seven or nine hours; the swelled cheek burst open and healed very fast. The woman had been laid up several days already on account of it. The family of Junkins lives in Nackenmixen, but Brecht and Gomber reside in and near Reading. Nackenmixen is in Bucks County. The four last mentioned were cured in the year 1819.

The daughter of John Arnold scalded herself with boiling coffee; the handle of the pot broke off while she was pouring out coffee, and the coffee ran over the arm and burnt it severely. I was present and witnessed the accident. I banished the burning; the arm did not get sore at all, and healed in a short time. This was in the year 1815. Mr. Arnold lived near Lebanon, Lebanon County, Penn.

JACOB STOUEFER, at Heckak, Bucks County, had a little child who was subject to convulsions every hour. I sold him a book containing the 25 letters; and he was persuaded by his neighbor, Henry Frankenfield, to try these 25 letters. The result was that the child was instantaneously free from convulsions and perfectly well. These letters are also found in this book.

If any one of the above named witnesses, who have been cured by me and my wife through the help of God, dares to call me a liar, and deny having been relieved by us, although they have confessed that they have been cured by us, I shall, if it is at all possible, compel them to repeat their confessions before a Justice of the Peace.

A letter to cure rheumatism, sold at from one to two dollars, and did not even give directions how to make use of it: these depending on verbal communications. John Allgaier, of Reading, had a very sore finger. I used sympathy to banish the wild-fire and to cure the finger. The very next morning the wild-fire was gone; he scarcely felt any pain, and the finger began to heal very fast. This was in 1819.

Gypsy Witch Book of Old Pennsylvania Dutch Pow-Wows and Hexes

This book is partly derived from a work published by a Gypsy, and partly from secret writings, and collected with much pain and trouble, from all parts of the world, at different periods, by the author, John George Hohman. I did not wish to publish it; my wife, also, was opposed to its publication; but my compassion for my suffering fellow-men was too strong, for I had seen many a one lose his entire sight by a wheal, and his life or limb by mortification. And how dreadfully has many a woman suffered from mother-fits? And I therefore ask thee again, oh friend, male or female, is it not to my everlasting praise, that I have had such books printed? Do I not deserve the rewards of God for it? Where else is the physician that could cure these diseases? Besides that I am a poor man in needy circumstances, and it is a help to me if I can make a little money with the sale of my books.

The Lord bless the beginning and the end of this little work, and be with us, that we may not misuse it, and thus commit a heavy sin! The word misuse, means as much as to use it for anything unnecessary. God bless us! Amen. The word Amen means as much as that the Lord might bring to pass in reality what had been asked for in prayer.

-NOTE-

There are many in America who believe neither in a hell nor in a heaven; but in Germany there are not so many of these persons found. I, Hohman, ask: Who can immediately banish the wheal, or mortification? I reply, and I, Hohman, say: All this is done by the Lord. Therefore, a hell and a heaven must exist; and I think very little of any one who dares deny it.

Gypsy Witch Book of Old Pennsylvania Dutch Pow-Wows and Hexes

JOHN GEORGE HOHMAN'S POW-WOWS ON ARTS AND REMEDIES

(1.) A good Remedy for Hysterics (or Mother Fits), to be used three times — Put that joint of the thumb which sits in the palm of the hand on the bare skin covering the small bone which stands out above the pit of the heart, and speak the following at the same time:

*Matrix, patrix, lay thyself right and safe,
Or thou or I shall on the third day fill the grave.* + + +

(2.) Another Remedy for Hysterics and for Colds. — This must be attended to every evening, that is, whenever you pull off your shoes and stockings, run your finger in between all the toes and smell it. This will certainly effect a cure.

(3.) A certain Remedy to stop Bleeding, which cures, no matter how far a person be away, if only his first name is rightly pronounced while using it:

*Jesus Christ, dearest blood!
That stoppeth the pain and stoppeth the blood.
In this help you [first name] God the Father, God the
Son, God the Holy Ghost. Amen.*

(4.) A remedy to be used when anyone is falling away, and which has cured many persons. — Let the person in perfect soberness and without having conversed with anyone, catch rain in a pot, before sunrise; boil an egg in this; bore three small holes in this egg with a needle, and carry it to an ant-hill made by big ants; and the person will feel relieved as soon as the egg is devoured.

(5.) Another Remedy to be applied when anyone is sick, which has affected many a cure where doctors could not help. — Let the sick person, without having conversed with anyone, put water in a bottle before sunrise, close it up tight, and put it immediately in some box or chest, lock it and stop up the keyhole; the key must be carried in one of the pockets for three days, as nobody dare have it except the person who puts the bottle with water in the chest or box.

(6.) A Good Remedy for Worms, to be Used for Men as Well as for Cattle:

> *Mary, God's Mother, traversed the land,*
> *Holding three worms close in her hand;*
> *One was white, the other was black, the third was red.*

This must be repeated three times, at the same time stroking the person or animal with the hand; and at the end of each application strike the back of the person or the animal, to wit: at the first application once, at the second application twice, and at the third application three times; and then set the worms a certain time, but not less than three minutes.

(7.) A Good Remedy Against Calumniation or Slander.

If you are calumniated or slandered to your very skin, to your very flesh, to your very bones, cast it back upon the false tongues. + + +

Take off your shirt, and turn it wrong side out, and then run your two thumbs along your body, close under the ribs, starting at the pit of the heart down to the thighs.

(8.) A Good Remedy for the Colic:

> *I warm ye, ye colic fiends! There is one sitting in judgment, who*
> *speaketh: just or unjust. Therefore*
> *beware, ye colic fiends!*
> *+ + +*

(9.) A Good Remedy for the Fever:

Good morning, dear Thursday! Take away from [name] the 77-fold fevers. Oh! thou dear Lord Jesus Christ, take them away from him!

+ + +

This must be used on Thursday for the first time, on Friday for the second time, and on Saturday for the third time; and each time thrice. The prayer of faith has also to be said each time, and not a word dare be spoken to anyone until the sun has risen. Neither dare the sick person speak to any one till after sunrise; nor eat pork, nor drink milk, nor cross running water, for nine days.

(10.) To Attach A Dog to A Person, Provided Nothing Else Was Used Before to Effect it.

Try to draw some of your blood, and let the dog eat it along with his food, and he will stay with you. Or scrape the four corners of your table while you are eating, and continue to eat with the same knife after having scraped the corners of the table. Let the dog eat those scrapings, and he will stay with you.

(11.) A Very Good Remedy For Palpitation of the Heart, and for Persons Who are Hide-Bound:

Palpitation and hide-bound, be off [name] ribs, Since Christ, our Lord, spoke truth with his lips.

(12.) A Precaution Against Injuries.

Whoever carries the right eye of a wolf fastened inside of his right sleeve, remains free from all injuries.

(13.) To Make A Wand for Searching for Iron, Ore, or Water.

On the first night of Christmas, between 11 and 12 o'clock, break off from any tree a young twig of one year's growth, in the three highest names (Father, Son and Holy Ghost), at the same time facing toward sunrise. Whenever you apply this wand in searching for anything, apply it three times. The twig must be forked, and each end of the fork must be held in one hand, so that the third and thickest part of it stands up, but do not hold it too tight. Strike the ground with the thickest end, and that which you desire will appear immediately, if there is any in the ground where you strike. The words to be spoken when the wand is thus applied are as follows:

Archangel Gabriel, I conjure thee in the name of God, the Almighty, to tell me, is there any water here or not? do tell me! + + +

If you are searching for Iron or Ore, you have to say the same, only mention the name of what you are searching for.

(14.) How to Obtain Things Which are Desired.

If you call upon another to ask for a favor, take care to carry a little of the five-finger grass with you, and you shall certainly obtain that you desired.

(15.) A Sure Way of Catching Fish.

Take rose seed and mustard seed, and the foot of a weasel, and hang these in a net, and the fish will certainly collect there.

(16.) A Safe Remedy for Various Ulcers, Boils, and other Defects.

Take the root of an iron-weed, and tie it around the neck; it cures running ulcers; it also serves against obstructions in the bladder (stranguary), and cures the piles, if the roots are boiled in water with honey, and drank; it cleans and heals the lungs and effects a good breath. If this root is planted among grape vines or fruit trees, it promotes the growth very much. Children who carry it are educated without any difficulty; they become fond of all useful arts and sciences, and grow up joyfully and cheerfully.

(17.) A Very Good Remedy for Mortification and Inflammation:

Sanctus Itorius res, call the rest. Here the mother of God came to his assistance, reaching out her snow-white hand, against the hot and cold brand. + + +

Make three crosses with the thumb. Everything which is applied in words, must be applied three times, and an interval of several hours must intervene each time, and for the third time it is to be applied the next day, unless where it is otherwise directed.

(18.) To Prevent Wicked or Malicious Persons from Doing You an Injury—Against Whom it is of Great Power:

*Dullix, ix, ux. Yea, you can't come over Pontio;
Pontio is above Pilato. + + +*

(19.) A Very Good Remedy to Destroy Bots or Worms in Horses.

You must mention the name of the horse, and say: "If you have any worms, I will catch you by the forehead. If they be white, brown or red, they shall and must now all be dead." You must shake the head of the horse three times, and pass your hand over his back three times to and fro. + + +

(20.) To Cure the Poll-Evil in Horses, in Two or Three Applications.

Break off three twigs from a cherry-tree: one towards morning, one towards evening, and one towards midnight. Cut three small pieces off the hind part of your shirt, and wrap each of those twigs in one of these pieces; then clean the poll-evil with the twigs and leave them under the eaves. The ends of the twigs which had been in the wound must be turned toward the north; after which you must do your business on them, that is to say, you must dirty them; then cover it, leaving the rags around the twigs. After all this the wound must be again stirred with the three twigs, in one or two days, and the twigs placed as before.

(21.) A Good Remedy for Bad Wounds and Burns:

The word of God, the milk of Jesus' mother, and Christ's blood, is for all wounds and burnings good. + + +

It is the safest way in all these cases to make the crosses with the hand or thumb three times over the affected parts; that is to say, over all those things to which the three crosses are attached.

(22.) A Very Good Remedy for the Wild-Fire:

*Wild-fire and the dragon, flew over a wagon.
The wild-fire abated and the dragon skated.*

(23.) To Stop Pains or Smarting in a Wound.

Cut three small twigs from a tree — each to be cut off in one cut — rub one end of each twig in the wound, and wrap them separately in a piece of white paper, and put them in a warm and dry place.

(24.) To Destroy Warts.

Roast chicken-feet and rub on warts; then bury them under the eaves.

(25.) To Banish the Whooping Cough.

Cut three small bunches of hair from the crown of the head of a child that has never seen its father; sew this hair up in an unbleached rag and hang it around the neck of the child having the whooping cough. The thread with which the rag is sewed must also be unbleached.

(26.) Another Good Remedy for the Whooping Cough.

Thrust the child having the whooping cough three times through a blackberry bush, without speaking or saying anything. The bush, however, must be grown fast at the two ends, and the child must be thrust through three times in the same manner, that is to say, from the same side it was thrust through in the first place.

(27.) A Good Remedy to Stop Bleeding:

Repeat these words three times:

> *This is the day on which the injury happened. Blood, thou must stop, until the Virgin Mary bring forth another son.*

(28.) A Good Remedy for the Toothache.

Stir the sore tooth with a needle until it draws blood; then take a thread and soak it with this blood. Then take vinegar and flour, mix them well so as to form a paste and spread it on a rag, then wrap this rag around the root of an apple-tree, and tie it very close with the above thread, after which the root must be well covered with ground.

(29. How to Walk and Step Securely in all Places:

Jesus walketh with [name]. He is my head; I am his limb. Therefore walketh Jesus with [name].

+ + +

(30.) A Very Good Remedy for the Colic.

Take half a gill of good rye whiskey, and a pipe full of tobacco; put the whiskey in a bottle, then smoke the tobacco and blow the smoke into the bottle, shake it well and drink it. This has cured the author of this book and many others. Or, take a white clay pipe which has turned blackish from smoking, pound it to a fine powder, and take it. This will have the same effect.

(31.) To Banish Convulsive Fevers.

Write the following letters on a piece of white paper, sew it on a piece of linen or muslin, and hang it around the neck until the fever leaves you:

```
Ab a x a C a t a b a x
Ab a x a C a t a b a x
Ab a x a C a t a b a
Ab a x a C a t a b
Ab a x a C a t a
Ab a x a C a t
Ab a x a C a
Ab a x a C
Ab a x a
Ab a x
Ab a
Ab
```

(32.) How to Banish the Fever.

Write the following words upon a paper and wrap it up in knot-grass, (breiten Megrieb,) and then tie it upon the body of the person who has the fever:

Potmat sineat,
Potmat sineat,
Potmat sineat.

(33.) A Very Good Plaster.

I doubt very much whether any physician in the United States can make a plaster equal to this. It heals the white swelling, and has cured the sore leg of a woman who for eighteen years had used the prescriptions of doctors in vain. Take two quarts of cider, one pound of bee's-wax, one pound of sheep-tallow, and one pound of tobacco; boil the tobacco in the cider till the strength is out, and then strain it, and add the other articles to the liquid: stir it over a gentle fire till all is dissolved.

(34.) To Make A Good Eye-Water.

Take four cents' worth of white vitriol, for cents' worth of prepared spicewort (calamus root), four cents' worth of cloves, a gill of good whiskey and a gill of water. Make the calamus fine and mix all together; then use it after it has stood a few hours.

(35.) A Very Good Remedy for the White Swelling.

Take a quart of unslacked {sic} lime, and pour two parts of water on it; stir it well and let it stand over night. The scum that collects on the lime-water must be taken off, and a pint of flax-seed oil poured in, after which it must be stirred until it becomes somewhat consistent: then put it in a pot or pan, and add a little lard and wax; melt it well, and make a plaster, and apply it to the parts affected — the plaster should be renewed every day, or at least every other day, until the swelling is gone.

(36.) **A Remedy for Epilepsy – Provided the Subject had Never Fallen into Fire or Water.**

Write reversely or backwards upon a piece of paper: *"IT IS ALL OVER!"* This is to be written but once upon the paper; then put it in a scarlet-red cloth, and then wrap it in a piece of unbleached linen, and hang it around the neck on the first Friday of the new moon. The thread with which it is tied must also be unbleached. + + +

(37.) **Remedy for Burns:**

"Burn, I blow on thee!" — *It must be blown on three times in the same breath, like the fire by the sun.* + + +

(38.) **To Stop Bleeding.**

Count backwards from fifty inclusive till you come down to three. As soon as you arrive at three, you will be done bleeding.

(39.) **A Remedy to Relieve Pain.**

Take a rag which was tied over a wound for the first time, and put it in water together with some copperas; but do not venture to stir the copperas until you are certain of the pain having left you.

(40.) **A Good Remedy For the Toothache.**

Cut out a piece of greensward (sod) in the morning before sunrise, quite unbeshrewdly from any place, breath three times upon it, and put it down upon the same place from which it was taken.

(41.) To Remove Bruises and Pains:

Bruise, thou shalt not heat;
Bruise, thou shalt not sweat;
Bruise, thou shalt not run,
No more than Virgin Mary shall bring forth
another son. + + +

(42.) A Remarkable Passage from the Work of Albertus Magnus.

It says: *If you burn a large frog to ashes, and mix the ashes with water, you will obtain an ointment that will, if put on any place covered with hair, destroy the hair and prevent it from growing again.*

(43.) Another Passage from the Work of Albertus Magnus.

If you find the stone which a vulture has in his knees, and which you may find by looking sharp, and put it in the victuals of two persons who hate each other, it causes them to make up and be good friends.

(44.) To Cure Fits or Convulsions.

You must go upon another person's land, and repeat the following words: *"I go before another court — I tie up my 77-fold fits."*

Then cut three small twigs off any tree on the land; in each twig you must make a knot. This must be done on a Friday morning before sunrise, in the decrease of the moon. + + + Then over your body where you feel the fits you make the crosses.

(45.) Cure for the Headache.

Tame thou flesh and bone, like Christ in Paradise; and who will assist thee, this I tell thee [name] for your repentance sake. + + +

This you must say three times, each time lasting for three minutes, and your headache will soon cease. But if your headache is caused by strong drink, or otherwise will not leave you soon, then you must repeat those words every minute. This, however, is not often necessary in regard to headache.

(46.) To Mend Broken Glass.

Take common cheese and wash it well, unslaked lime and the white of eggs, rub all these well together until it becomes one mass, and then use it. If it is made right, it will certainly hold.

(47.) How to Make Cattle Return to the Same Place.

Pull out three small bunches of hair, one between the horns, one from the middle of the back, and one near the tail, and make your cattle eat it in their feed.

(48.) Another Method of Making Cattle Return Home.

Take a handful of salt, go upon your fields and make your cattle walk three times around the same stump or stone, each time keeping the same direction; that is to say, you must three times arrive at the same end of the stump or stone at which you started from, and then let your cattle lick the salt from the stump or stone.

(49.) To Prevent the Hessian Fly from Injuring Wheat.

Take pulverized charcoal, make ley of it, and soak the seed wheat in it; take it out of the ley, and on every bushel of wheat sprinkle a quart of urine; stir it well, then spread it out to dry.

(50.) To Prevent Cherries from Ripening Before Martinmas.

Engraft the twigs upon a mulberry-tree, and your desire is accomplished.

(51.) Stinging Nettles — Good for Banishing Fears and Fancies, and to Cause Fish to Collect.

Whenever you hold this weed in your hand together with Millifolia, you are safe from all fears and fancies that frequently deceive men. If you mix it with a decoction of the hemlock, and rub your hands with it, and put the rest in water that contains fish, you will find the fish to collect around your hands. Whenever you pull your hands out of the water, the fish disappear by returning to their former places.

(52.) Heliotrope (Sunflower), A Means to Prevent Calumniation.

The virtues of this plant are miraculous. If it be collected in the sign of the lion, in the month of August, and wrapped up in a laurel leaf together with the tooth of a wolf. Whoever carries this about him, will never be addressed harshly by anyone, but all will speak to him kindly and peaceably. And if anything has been stolen from you put this under your head during the night, and you will surely see the whole figure of the thief. This has been found true.

(53.) To Heal A Sore Mouth.

If you have the scurvy or quinsy too, I breathe my breath three times into you.

+ + +

(54.) A Good Remedy for Consumption.

Consumption, I order thee out of the bones into the flesh, out of the flesh upon the skin, out of the skin into the wilds of the forest.

+ + +

(55.) Swallow-Wort.

A means to overcome and end all fighting and anger, and to cause a sick man to weep when his health is restored, or to sing with a cheerful voice when on his death bed; also a very good remedy for dim eyes or shining of the eyes. This weed grows at the time when the swallows build their nests or eagles breed. If a man carries this about him, together with the heart of a mole, he shall overcome all fighting and anger. If these things are put upon the head of a sick man, he shall weep at the restoration of his health, and sing with a cheerful voice when he comes to die. When the swallow-wort blooms, the flowers must be pounded up and boiled, and then the water must be poured off into another vessel, and again be placed to the fire and carefully skimmed; then it must be filtered through a cloth and preserved, and whosoever has dim eyes or shining eyes, may bathe his eyes with it, and they will become clear and sound.

(56.) For the Hollow Horn in Cows.

Bore a small hole in the hollow horn, milk the same cow, and squirt her milk into the horn; this is the best cure. Use a syringe to squirt the milk into the horn.

(57.) A Very Good and Certain Means of Destroying the Wheal in the Eye.

Take a dirty plate; if you have none, you can easily dirty one, and the person for whom you are using sympathy shall in a few minutes find the pain much relieved. You must hold that side of the plate or dish, which is used in eating, toward the eye. While you hold the plate before the eye, you must say:

Dirty plate, I press thee,
Wheal in the eye, do flee.
+ + +

(58.) To Make Chickens Lay Many Eggs.

Take the dung of rabbits, pound it to powder, mix it with bran, wet the mixture till it forms lumps, and feed your chickens with it, and they will keep on laying a great many eggs.

(59.) Words to be Spoken While Making Divinatory Wands.

In making divinatory wands, they must be broken as before directed, and while breaking and before using them, the following words must be spoken:

Divining rod, do thou keep that power, Which God gave unto thee at the very first hour.

(60.) How to Destroy a Tape-Worm.

Worm, I conjure thee by the living God, that thou shalt flee this blood and this flesh, like as God the Lord will shun that judge who judges unjustly, although he might have judged aright.
+ + +

(61.) A Good Remedy for the Bots in Horses.

Every time you use this, you must stroke the horse down with the hand three times, and lead it about three times holding its head toward the sun, saying: *"The Holy One saith: Joseph passed over a field and there he found three small worms; the one being black, another being brown, and the third being red; thou shalt die and be dead."*

(62.) How to Cure a Burn:

Three holy men went out walking,
They did bless the heat and the burning;
They blessed that it might not increase;
They blessed that it might quickly cease!
+ + +

(63.) To Cure the Bite of a Snake:

God has created all things and they were good;
Thou only, serpent, art damned,
Cursed be thou and thy sting. + + +
Zing, zing, zing!

(64.) Security Against Mad Dogs.

Dog, hold thy nose to the ground,
God has made me and thee, hound!
+ + +

This you must repeat in the direction of the dog; and the three crosses you must make toward the dog, and the words must be spoken before he sees you.

(65.) To Remove Pain and Heal up Wounds with Three Switches.

*With this switch and Christ's dear blood,
I banish your pain and do you good!*
+ + +

Mind it well: you must in one cut, sever from a tree, a young branch pointing toward sunrise, and then make three pieces of it, which you successively put in the wound. Holding them in your hand, you take the one toward your right side first. Everything prescribed in this book must be used three times, even if the three crosses should not be affixed. Words are always to have an interval of half an hour, and between the second and third time should pass a whole night, except where it is other wise directed. The above three sticks, after the end of each has been put into the wound as before directed, must be put in a piece of white paper, and placed where they will be warm and dry.

(66.) Remedy for Fever, Worms, and the Colic:

*Jerusalem, thou Jewish city,
In which Christ our Lord, was born,
Thou shalt turn into water and blood,
Because it is for [name] fever, worms, and colic good.*

(67.) How to Cure Weakness of the Limbs.

Take the buds of the birch tree or the inner bark of the root of the tree at the time of the budding of the birch, and make a tea of it, and drink it occasionally through the day. Yet, after having used it for two weeks, it must be discontinued for a while, before it is resorted to again; and during the two weeks of its use it is well at times to use water for a day instead of the tea.

(68.) Another Remedy for Weakness.

Take Bittany and St. John's Wort, and put them in good old rye whiskey. To drink some of this in the morning before having taken anything else, is very wholesome and good. A tea made of the acorns of the white oak is very good for weakness of the limbs.

(69.) To Make Horses That Refuse Their Feed to Eat Again — Especially Applicable When They are Afflicted in This Manner on the Public Roads.

Open the jaws of the horse, which refuses his feed, and knock three times on his palate. This will certainly cause the horse to eat again without hesitation, and to go along willingly.

(70.) A Good Method of Destroying Rats and Mice.

Every time you bring grain into your barn, you must, in putting down the three first sheaves, repeat the following words:

"Rats and mice, these three sheaves I give to you, in order that you may not destroy any of my wheat."

The name of the kind of grain must also be mentioned.

(71.) To Cure Any Excrescence or Wen on a Horse.

Take any bone which you accidentally find, for you dare not be looking for it, and rub the wen of the horse with it, always bearing in mind that it must be done in the decreasing moon, and the wen will certainly disappear. The bone, however, must be replaced as it was lying before.

(72.) How to Prepare a Good Eye-Water.

Take one ounce of white vitriol and one ounce of sugar of lead, dissolve them in oil of rosemary, and put it in a quart bottle, which you fill up with rose-water. Bathe the eyes with it night and morning.

(73.) How to Cause Male or Female Thieves to Stand Still Without Being Able to Move Forward or Backward.

In using any prescription of this book in regard to making others stand still, it is best to be walking about; and repeat the following three times:

"Oh, Peter, oh Peter, borrow the power from God; what I shall bind with the bands of a Christian hand, shall be bound; all male and female thieves, be they great or small, young or old, shall be spellbound, by the power of God, and not be able to walk forward or backward until I see them with my eyes, and give them leave with my tongue, except it be that they count for me all the stones that may be between heaven and earth, all rain-drops, all the leaves and all the grasses in the world. This I pray for the repentance of my enemies."

+ + +

Repeat your articles of faith and the Lord's Prayer.

If the thieves are to remain alive, the sun dare not shine upon them before their release. There are two ways of releasing them, which will be particularly stated: The first is this that you tell them, in the name of St. John, to leave; the other is as follows: *"The words which have bound thee shall give thee free."*

+ + +

(74.) To Cure the Sweeney in Horses.

Take a piece of old bacon, and cut it into small pieces, put them in a pan and roast them well, put in a handful of fish-worms, a gill of oats and three spoonfuls of salt into it; roast the whole of this until it turns black, and then filter it through a cloth; after which you put a gill of soft soap, half a gill of rye whiskey, half a gill of vinegar, and half a pint of rain-water to it; mix it well, and smear it over the part affected with sweeney on the third, the sixth, and the ninth day of the new moon, and warm it with an oaken board.

(75.) How to Make Molasses.

Take pumpkins, boil them, press the juice out of them, and boil the juice to a proper consistence. There is nothing else necessary. The author of this book, John George Hohman, has tasted this molasses, thinking it was the genuine kind, until the people of the house told him what it was.

(76.) To Make Good Beer.

Take a handful of hops, five or six gallons of water, about three tablespoonfuls of ginger, half a gallon of molasses; filter the water, hops and ginger into a tub containing the molasses.

(77.) Cure for the Epilepsy.

Take a turtle dove, cut its throat, and let the person afflicted with epilepsy, drink the blood.

(78.) Another Way to Make Cattle Return Home.

Feed your cattle out of a pot or kettle used in preparing your dinner, and they will always return to your stable.

(79.) A Very Good Remedy to Cure Sores.

Boil the bulbs (roots) of the white lily in cream, and put it on the sore in the form of a plaster. Southern-Wort has the same effect.

(80.) A Good Cure for Wounds.

Take the bones of a calf, and burn them until they turn to powder, and then strew it into the wound. The powder prevents the flesh from putrefying, and is therefore of great importance in healing the wound.

(81.) To Make Oil out of Paper which is Good for Sore Eyes.

A man from Germany informed me that to burn two sheets of white paper would produce about three drops of oil or water, which would heal all sores in or about the eye if rubbed with it. Any affection of the eyes can be cured in this way, as long as the apple of the eye is sound.

(81.) To Destroy Crab-Lice.

Take capuchin powder, mix it with hog's lard, and smear yourself with it. Or boil cammock, and wash the place where the lice keep themselves.

(83.) To Prevent the Worst Kind of Paper from Blotting.

Dissolve alum in water, and put it on the paper, and I, Hohman, would like to see who cannot write on it, when it is dried.

(84.) A Very Good Remedy for the Gravel.

The author of this book, John George Hohman, applied this remedy, and soon felt relieved. I knew a man who could find no relief from the medicine of any doctor; he then used the following remedy, to wit: he ate every morning seven peach-stones before tasting anything else, which relieved him very much; but as he had the gravel very bad, he was obliged to use it constantly. I, Hohman, have used it for several weeks. I still feel a touch of it now and then, yet I had it so badly that I cried out aloud every time that I had to make water. I owe a thousand thanks to God and the person who told me of this remedy.

(85.) A Good Remedy for Those Who Cannot Keep Their Water.

Burn a hog's bladder to powder, and take it inwardly.

(86.) To Remove a Wen During the Crescent Moon.

Look over the wen, directly towards the moon, and say:

> *"Whatever grows does grow; and whatever diminishes, does diminish."*

This must be said three times in the same breath.

(87.) To Destroy Field-Mice and Moles.

Put unslaked lime in their holes and they will disappear.

(88.) To Remove a Scum or Skin From the Eye.

Before sunrise on St. Bartholomew's Day, you must dig up four or five roots of the dandelion weed, taking good care to get the ends of the roots; then you must procure a rag and a thread that have never been in the water; the thread, which dare not have a single knot in it, is used in sewing up the roots into the rag, and the whole is then to be hung before the eye until the scum disappears. The tape by which it is fastened must never have been in the water,

(89.) For Deafness, Roaring or Buzzing in the Ear, and for Toothache.

A few drops of refined camphor-oil put upon cotton, and thus applied to the aching tooth, relives very much. When put in the ear it strengthens the hearing and removes the roaring and whizzing in the same.

(90.) A Good Way to Cause Children to Cut Their Teeth Without Pain.

Boil the brain of a rabbit and rub the gums of the children with it, and their teeth will grow without pain to them.

(91.) Vomiting and Diarrhea.

Take pulverized cloves and eat them together with bread soaked in red wine, and you will soon find relief. The cloves may be put upon the bread.

(92.) To Heal Burns.

Pound or press the juice of male fern, and put it on the burnt spots and they will heal very fast. Better yet, however, if you smear the above juice upon a rag, and put it on like a plaster.

(93.) Very Good Cure for Weakness of the Limbs, for the Purification of the Blood, for the Invigorating of the Head and Hear, and to Remove Giddiness, Etc.

Take two drops of oil of cloves in a tablespoonful of white wine early in the morning, and before eating anything else. This is also good for the mother-pains and the colic. The oil of cloves which you buy in the drug stores will answer the purpose. These remedies are also applicable to cure the cold when it settles in the bowels, and to stop vomiting. A few drops of this oil poured upon cotton and applied to the aching teeth, relieves the pain.

(94.) For Dysentery and Diarrhea.

Take the moss off of trees, and boil it in red wine, and let those who are affected with those diseases drink it.

(95.) Cure for the Toothache.

Hohman, the author of this book, has cured the severest toothache more than sixty times, with this remedy, and, out of the sixty times he applied it, it failed but once in affecting a cure. Take blue vitriol and put a piece of it in the hollow tooth, yet not too much; spit out the water that collects in the mouth, and be careful to swallow none. I do not know whether it is good for teeth that are not hollow, but I should judge it would cure any kind of toothache.

(96.) Advice to Pregnant Women.

Pregnant women must be very careful not to use any camphor; and no camphor should be administered to those women who have the mother-fits.

Gypsy Witch Book of Old Pennsylvania Dutch Pow-Wows and Hexes

(97.) Cure for the Bite of a Mad Dog.

A certain Mr. Valentine Kittering, of Dauphin County, has communicated to the Senate of Pennsylvania a sure remedy for the bite of any kind of mad animals. He says that his ancestors had already used it in Germany 250 years ago, and that he had always found it to answer the purpose, during a residence of fifty years in the United States. He only published it from motives of humanity.

This remedy consists in the weed called Chick-weed. It is a summer plant, known to the Germans and Swiss by the names of Gauchneil, Rothea Meyer, or Rother Huehnerdarm. In England it is called Red Pimpernel; and its botanical name is Angelica Phonicea. It must be gathered in June when in full bloom and dried in the shade, and then pulverized. The dose of this for a grown person is a small tablespoonful, or in weight a drachm and a scruple, at once, in beer or water. For children the dose is the same, yet it must be administered at three different times. In applying it to animals, it must be used green, cut to pieces and mixed with bran or other feed. For the hogs the pulverized weed is made into little balls by mixing it with flour and water. It can also be put on bread and butter, or in honey, molasses, etc. The Rev. Henry Muhlenberg says that in Germany 30 grains of this powder are given four times a day, the first day, then one dose a day for a whole week; while at the same time the wound is washed out with a decoction of the weed, and then the powder strewed in it. Mr. Kittering says that he in all instances administered but one dose, with the most happy results. This is said to be the same remedy through which the late Doctor William Stoy effected so many cures.

(98.) A Very Good Means to Increase the Growth of Wool on Sheep and to Prevent Disease Among Them.

William Ellis, in his excellent work on the English manner of raising sheep, relates the following: I know a tenant who had a flock of sheep that produced an unusual quantity of wool. He informed me that he was in the habit of washing his sheep with buttermilk just after shearing them, which was the cause of the unusual growth of wool; because it is a known fact that buttermilk does not only improve the growth of sheep's wool, but also the hair of other animals. Those who have no buttermilk may substitute common milk, mixed with salt and water, which will answer nearly as well to wash the sheep just sheared. And I guarantee that by rightly applying this means, you will not only have a great increase of wool, but the sheep-lice and their entire brood will be destroyed. It also cures all manner of scab and itch, and prevents them from taking cold.

(99.) A Well-Tried Plaster to Remove Mortification.

Take six hen's eggs and boil them in hot ashes until they are right hard; then take the yellow of the eggs and fry them in a gill of lard until they are quite black; then put a handful of rue with it, and afterward filter it through a cloth. When this is done add a gill of sweet oil to it. It will take most effect where the plaster for a female is prepared by a male, and the plaster for a male prepared by a female.

(100.) A Good Remedy for the Poll-Evil in Horses.

Take white turpentine, rub it over the poll-evil with your hand, and then melt it with a hot iron, so that it runs into the wound. After this take Neatsfoot oil or goose grease and rub it into the wound in the same manner, and for three days in succession, commencing on the last Friday of the last quarter of the moon.

(101.) For the Scurvy and Sore Throat.

Speak the following, and it will certainly help you:

Job went through the land, holding his staff close in the hand, when God the Lord did meet him, and said to him: Job, what art thou grieved at? Job said: Oh God, why should I not be sad? My throat and my mouth are rotting away. Then said the Lord to Job: In yonder valley there is a well which will cure thee [name], and thy mouth, and thy throat, in the name of God the Father, the Son and the Holy Ghost. Amen.

This must be spoken three times in the morning and three times in the evening; and where it reads "which will cure," you must blow three times in the child's mouth.

(102.) A Very Good Plaster.

Take wormwood, rue, meddles, sheeprip-wort, pointy plantain, in equal proportions, a larger proportion of bees'-wax and tallow, and some spirits of turpentine; put it together in a pot, boil it well, and then strain it, and you have a very good plaster.

(103.) To Stop Bleeding:

I walk through a green forest;
There I find three wells, cool and cold;
The first is called courage,
The second is called good,
And the third is called stop the blood.

+ + +

(104.) Another Way to Stop Bleeding and to Heal Wounds in Man as well as Animals.

On Christ's grave there grows three roses; the first is kind, the second is valued among the rulers, and the third says: blood, thou must stop, and wound, thou must heal. Everything prescribed for man in this book is also applicable to animals.

(105.) For Gaining a Lawful Suit.

It reads, if anyone has to settle any just claim by way of a law suit let him take some of the largest kind of sage and write the name of the twelve apostles on the leaves, and put them in his shoes before entering the courthouse, and he shall certainly gain the suit.

(106.) For the Swelling of Cattle:

To Desh break no Flesh, but to Desh! While saying this, run your hand along the back of the animal.
+ + +

NOTE. — The hand must be put upon the bare skin in all cases of using sympathetic words.

(107.) An Easy Method of Catching Fish.

In a vessel of white glass must be put: 8 grains of civit, (musk), and as much castorium; two ounces of eel-fat, and 4 ounces of unsalted butter; after which the vessel must be well closed, and put in some place where it will keep moderately warm for nine or ten days, and then the composition must be well stirred with a stick until it is perfectly mixed.

APPLICATION — 1. In using the hooks. — Worms or insects used for baiting the hooks must first be moistened with this composition, and then put in a bladder or box, which may be carried in the pocket.

2. In using the net. — Small balls formed of the soft part of fresh bread must be dipped in this composition and then by means of thread fastened inside of the net before throwing it into the water.

3. Catching Fish with the hand. — Besmear your legs or boots with this composition before entering the water at the place where the fish are expected, and they will collect in great numbers around you.

(108.) A Very Good and Safe Remedy for Rheumatism.

From one to two dollars have often been paid for this recipe alone, it being the best and surest remedy to cure the rheumatism. Let it be known therefore: Take a piece of cloth, some tape and thread, neither of which must ever have been in water; the thread must not have a single knot in it, and the cloth and tape must have been spun by a child not quite or at least not more than seven years of age. The letter given below must be carefully sewed in the piece of cloth, and tied around the neck, unbeshrewdly; on the first Friday in the decreasing moon; and immediately after hanging it around the neck, the Lord's Prayer and the articles of faith must be repeated. What now follows must be written in the before-mentioned letter:

"May God the Father, Son and Holy Ghost grant it. Amen. Seek immediately, and seek; thus commandeth the Lord thy God, through the first man whom God did love upon earth. Seek immediately, and seek; thus commandeth the Lord thy God, through Luke, the Evangelist, and through Paul, the Apostle. Seek immediately, and seek; thus commandeth the Lord thy God, through the twelve messengers. Seek immediately, and seek; thus commandeth the Lord thy God by the first man that God might be loved. Seek immediately, and convulse; thus commandeth the Lord thy God, through the Holy Fathers, who have been made by divine and holy writ. Seek immediately, and convulse; thus commandeth the Lord thy God, through the dear and holy angels, and through his paternal and Divine Omnipotence, and his heavenly confidence and endurance. Seek immediately, and convulse; thus commandeth the Lord thy God, through the burning oven which was preserved by the blessing of God. Seek immediately, and convulse; thus commandeth the Lord thy God, through all power and might, through the prophet Jonah who was preserved in the belly of the whale for three days and three nights, by the blessing of God. Seek immediately, and convulse; thus commandeth the Lord thy God, through all the power and might which proceed from divine humility, and in all-eternity; whereby no harm be done unto + N + nor unto any part of his body be they the ravenous convulsions, or

the yellow convulsions, or the white convulsions, or the red convulsions, or the black convulsions, or by whatever name convulsions may be called; these all shall do no harm unto thee + N + nor to any part of thy body, nor to thy head, nor to thy neck, nor to thy heart, nor to thy stomach, nor to any of thy veins, nor to thy arms, nor to thy legs, nor to thy eyes, nor to thy tongue, nor to any part or parcel of thy body. This I write for thee + N + in these words, and in the name of God the Father, Son and Holy Ghost. Amen. God bless it. Amen."

Notice — If anyone should write such a letter for another, the Christian name of the person must be mentioned in it; as you will observe, where the N stands singly in the above letter, there must be the name.

(109.) A Good Way to Destroy Worms in Bee-Hives.

With very little trouble and at the expense of a quarter dollar, you can certainly free your bee-hives from worms for a whole year. Get from an apothecary store the powder called Pensses Blum, which will not injure the bees in the least. The application of it is as follows: For one bee-hive you take as much of this powder as the point of your knife will hold, mix it with one ounce of good whiskey, and put it in a common vial; then make a hole in the bee-hive and pour it in thus mixed with the whiskey, which is sufficient for one hive at once. Make the hole so that it can be easily poured in. As said before, a quarter dollar's worth of this powder is enough for one hive.

(110.) Recipe for Making a Paste to Prevent Gun-Barrels from Rusting whether Iron or Steel.

Take an ounce of bear's fat, half an ounce of badger's grease, half an ounce of snake's fat, one ounce of almond oil, and a quarter of an ounce of pulverized indigo, and melt it altogether in a new vessel over a fire, stir it well, and put it afterward into some vessel. In using it, a lump as large as a common nut must be put upon a piece of woolen cloth and then rubbed on the barrel and lock of the gun, and it will keep the barrel from rusting.

(111.) To Make a Wick Which is Never Consumed.

Take an ounce of asbestos and boil it in a quart of strong lye for two hours; then pour off the lye and clarify what remains by pouring rain-water on it three or four times, after which you can form a wick from it which will never be consumed by the fire.

(112.) A Morning Prayer to be Spoken Before Starting on a Journey Which Will Save the Person From All Mishaps:

I (here the name is to be pronounced) will go on a journey to-day; I will walk upon God's way, and walk where God himself did walk, and our dear Lord Jesus Christ, and our dearest Virgin with her dear little babe, with her seven rings and her true things. Oh, thou! my dear Lord Jesus Christ, I am thine own, that no dog may bite me, no wolf bite me, and no murderer secretly approach me; save me, O my God, from sudden death! I am in God's hands, and there I will bind myself. In God's hands I am by our Lord Jesus' five wounds, that any gun or other arms may not do me any more harm than the virginity of our Holy Virgin Mary was injured by the favor of her beloved Jesus. After this say three Lord's prayers, the Ave Maria, and the articles of faith.

Gypsy Witch Book of Old Pennsylvania Dutch Pow-Wows and Hexes

The bright patterns and geometric forms, known as Hex Signs, were used by the ancestors of the Pennsylvania German settlers on barns, birth certificates, furniture, pottery, etc. Many are thought to have come originally from religious motif designs, the two main patterns being the Sun and Tree of Life.

(113.) A Safe and Approved Means to be Applied in Cases of Fire and Pestilence:

Welcome, thou fiery fiend! Do not extend further than thou already hast. This I count unto thee as a repentant act, in the name of God the Father, the Son and the Holy Ghost.

I command unto thee, fire, by the power of God, which createth and worketh everything, that thou now do cease, and not extend any further as certainly as Christ was standing on the Jordan's stormy banks, being baptized by John the holy man.

This I count unto thee as a repentant act in the name of the holy Trinity.

I command unto thee, fire, by the power of God, now to abate thy flames; as certainly as Mary retained her virginity before all ladies who retained theirs, so chaste and pure; therefore, fire, cease thy wrath.

This I count unto thee as a repentant act in the name of the holy Trinity.

I command unto thee, fire, to abate thy heat, by the precious blood of Jesus Christ, which he has shed for us, and our sins and transgressions.

This I count unto thee, fire, as a repentant act, in the name of God the Father, the Son and the Holy Ghost.

Jesus of Nazareth, a king of the Jews, help us from this dangerous fire, and guard this land and its bounds from all epidemic disease and pestilence.

REMARKS — This has been discovered by a Christian Gypsy King of Egypt. Anno 1740, on the 10th of June, six gypsies were executed on the gallows in the kingdom of Prussia. The seventh of their party was a man of eighty years of age and was to be executed by the sword on the 16th of the same month. But fortunately for him, quite unexpectedly, a conflagration broke out, and the old Gypsy was taken to the fire to try his arts, which he successfully did to the great surprise of all present, by bespeaking the conflagration in a manner that it wholly or entirely ceased and disappeared in less than ten minutes. Upon this, the proof having been given in daytime, he received pardon and was set at liberty. This was confirmed and attested by the government of the King of Prussia, and the General Superintendent at Koenigsberg, and given to the public in print. It was first published at Koenigsberg in Prussia, by Alexander Bausman, Anno 1745.

Whoever has this letter in his house will be free from all danger of fire, as well as from lightning. If a pregnant woman carries this letter about her, neither enchantment nor evil spirits can injure her or her child. Further, if anybody has this letter in his house, or carries it about his person, he will be safe from the injuries of pestilence.

While saying these sentences, one must pass three times around the fire. This has availed in all instances.

(114.) To Prevent Conflagration.

Take a black chicken, in the morning or evening, cut its head off and throw it upon the ground; cut its stomach out, yet leave it altogether; then try to get a piece of a shirt which was worn by a chaste virgin during her terms, and cut out a piece as large as a common dish from that part which is bloodiest. These two things wrap up together, then try to get an egg which was laid on maunday{sic}Thursday. These three things put together in wax; then put them in a pot holding eight quarts, and bury it under the threshold of your house, with the aid of God, and as long as there remains a single stick of your house together, no conflagration will happen. If your house should happen to be on fire already in front and behind, the fire will nevertheless do no injury to you nor to your children. This is done by the power of God, and is quite certain and infallible. If fire should break out unexpectedly, then try to get a whole shirt in which your servant-maid had her terms or a sheet on which a child was born, and throw it into the fire, wrapped up in a bundle, and without saying anything. This will certainly stop it.

(115.) To Prevent Witches from Bewitching Cattle, to be Written and Placed in the Stable; and Against Bad Men and Evil Spirits which Nightly Torment Old and Young People, to be Written and Placed on the Bedstead:

"Trotter Head, I forbid thee my house and premises; I forbid thee my horse and cow-stable; I forbid thee my bedstead, that thou mayest not breathe upon me; breathe into some other house, until thou hast ascended every hill, until thou hast counted every fence-post, and until thou hast crossed every water. And thus dear day may come again into my house, in the name of God the Father, the Son, and the Holy Ghost. Amen."

This will certainly protect and free all persons and animals from witchcraft.

(116.) To Extinguish Fire Without Water.

Write the following words on each side of a plate, and throw it into the fire, and it will be extinguished forthwith:

```
    S A T O R           O P E R A
    A R E P O           R O T A S
       T E N E T
```

(117.) To Prevent Bad People from Getting About the Cattle.

Take wormwood, gith, five-finger weed, and assafoetida; three cents' worth of each; the straw of horse beans, some dirt swept together behind the door of the stable and a little salt. Tie these all up together with a tape, and put the bundle in a hole about the threshold over which your cattle pass in and out, and cover it well with lignum-vitae wood. This will certainly be of use.

(118.) Another Method of Stopping Fire:

Our dear Sarah journeyed through the land, having a fiery hot brand in her hand. The fiery brand heats; the fiery brand sweats. Fiery brand, stop your heat; fiery brand, stop your sweat.

(119.) **How to Fasten or Spell-Bind Anything.**

You say, *"Christ's cross and Christ's crown, Christ Jesus' colored blood, be thou every hour good. God, the Father, is before me; God, the Son, is beside me; God, the Holy Ghost, is behind me. Whoever now is stronger than these three persons may come, by day or night, to attack me."* + + +

Then say the Lord's Prayer three times.

(120.) **Another Way of Fastening or Spell-Binding.**

After repeating the above, you speak, *"At every step may Jesus walk with (name). He is my head; I am his limb; therefore, Jesus, be with (name)."*

(121.) **A Benediction to Prevent Fire.**

"The bitter sorrows and the death of our dear Lord Jesus Christ shall prevail. Fire and wind and great heat and all that is within the power of these elements, I command thee, through the Lord Jesus Christ, who has spoken to the winds and the waters, and they obeyed him. By these powerful words spoken by Jesus, I command, threaten, and inform thee, fire, flame, and heat, and your powers as elements, to flee forthwith. The holy, rosy blood of our dear Lord Jesus Christ may rule it.

Thou, fire, and wind, and great heat, I command thee, as the Lord did, by his holy angels, command the great heat in the fiery oven to leave those three holy men, Shadrach and his companions, Meshach and Abednego, untouched, which was done accordingly. Thus thou shalt abate, thou fire, flame, and great heat, the Almighty God having spoken in creating the four elements, together with heaven and earth; Fiat! Fiat! Fiat! that is: It shall be in the name of God the Father, the Son, and the Holy Ghost. Amen."

(122.) How to Relieve Persons or Animals after being Bewitched.

"Three false tongues have bound thee, three holy tongues have spoken for thee. The first is God the Father, the second is God the Son, and the third is God the Holy Ghost. They will give you blood and flesh, peace and comfort. Flesh and blood are grown upon thee, born on thee, and lost on thee. If any man trample on thee with his horse, God will bless thee, and the holy Ciprian; has any woman trampled on thee, God and the body of Mary shall bless thee; if any servant has given you trouble, I bless thee through God and the laws of heaven; if any servant-maid or woman has led you astray, God and the heavenly constellations shall bless thee. Heaven is above thee, the earth is beneath thee, and thou art between. I bless thee against all bramplings{sic} by horses. Our dear Lord Jesus Christ walked about in his bitter afflictions and death; and all the Jews that had spoken and promised, trembled in their falsehoods and mockery. Look, now trembleth the Son of God, as if he had the itch, said the Jews. And then spake Jesus: I have not the itch and no one shall have it. Whoever will assist me to carry the cross, him will I free from the itch, in the name of God the Father, the Son, and the Holy Ghost. Amen."

(123.) To Protect Houses and Premises Against Sickness and Theft.

Ito, alto Massa Dandi Bando, III. Amen

J. R. N. R. J.
Our Lord Jesus Christ stepped into the hall, and the Jews searched him everywhere. Thus shalt those who now speak evil of me with their false tongues, and contend against me, one day bear sorrows, be silenced, dumbstruck, intimidated, and abused, forever and ever, by the glory of God. The glory of God shall assist me in this. Do thou aid me J. J. J. forever and ever. Amen."

(124.) Against Mishaps and Dangers in the House.

Sanct Matheus, Sanct Marcus, Sanct Lucas, Sanct Johannis.

(125.) A Direction for a Gypsy Sentence, to be Carried About the Person as a Protection Under all Circumstances.

Like unto the prophet Jonas, as a type of Christ, who was guarded for three days and three nights in the belly of a whale, thus shall the Almighty God, as a Father, guard and protect me from all evil. J. J. J.

(126.) Against Evil Spirits and all Manner of Witchcraft.

I.
N. I. R.
I.
SANCTUS SPIRITUS.
I.
N. I. R.
I.

All this be guarded here in time, and there in eternity. Amen.

You must write all the above on a piece of white paper and carry it about you. The characters or letters above signify: *"God bless me here in time, and there eternally."*

(127.) Against Swellings:

"Three pure virgins went out on a journey to inspect a swelling and sickness. The first one said, It is hoarse. The second said, It is not. The third said, If it is not, then will our Lord Jesus Christ come."

This must be spoken in the name of the Holy Trinity.

(128.) How to Treat a Cow After the Milk is Taken from Her.

Give to the cow three spoonfuls of her last milk, and say to the spirits in her blood:

"Ninny has done it, and I have swallowed her in the name of God the Father, the Son, and the Holy Ghost. Amen."

Pray what you choose at the same time.

(129.) Against Adversities and all Manner of Contention:

Power, hero, Prince of Peace, J. J. J.

(130.) Against Danger and Death, to be Carried About the Person:

I know that my Redeemer liveth, and that he will call me from the grave, ect.

(131.) Another Method of Treating a Sick Cow.

J. The cross of Jesus Christ poured out milk;
J. The cross of Jesus Christ poured out water;
J. The cross of Jesus Christ has poured them out;

These lines must be written on three pieces of white paper; then take the milk of the sick cow and these three pieces of paper, put them in a pot, and scrape a little of the skull of a criminal; close it well, and put it over a hot fire, and the witch will have to die. If you take the three pieces of paper, with the writing on them, in your mouth and go out before your house, speak three times, and then give them to your cattle, you shall not only see all the witches, but your cattle will also get well again.

(132.) Against the Fever.

Pray early in the morning, and then turn your shirt around the left sleeve, and say: *"Turn, thou, shirt, and thou, fever, do likewise turn. (Do not forget to mention the name of the person having the fever.) This, I tell thee, for thy repentance sake, in the name of God the Father, the Son, and the Holy Ghost. Amen."* If you repeat this for three successive mornings the fever will disappear.

(133.) To Spell-Bind A Thief so that He Cannot Stir.

This benediction must be spoken on a Thursday morning, before sunrise and in the open air:

"Thus shall rule it, God the Father, the Son, and the Holy Ghost. Amen. Thirty-three Angels speak to each other coming to administer in company with Mary. Then spoke dear Daniel, the holy one: Trust, my dear woman, I see some thieves coming who intend stealing your dear babe; this I cannot conceal from you. Then spake our dear Lady to Saint Peter; I have bound with a band, through

Christ's hand; therefore, my thieves are bound even by the hand of Christ, if they wish to steal mine own, in the house, in the chest, upon the meadow or fields, in the woods, in the orchard, in the vineyard, or in the garden, or wherever they intend to steal. Our dear Lady said: Whoever chooses may steal; yet if anyone does steal, he shall stand like a buck, he shall stand like a stake, and shall count all the stones upon the earth, and all the stars in the heavens. Thus I give thee leave, and command every spirit to be master over every thief, by the guardianship of Saint Daniel, and by the burden of this world's goods. And the countenance shall be unto thee, that thou canst not move from the spot, as long as my tongue in the flesh shall not give thee leave. This I command thee by the Holy Virgin Mary, the Mother of God, by the power and might by which he has created heaven and earth, by the host of all the angels, and by all the saints of God the Father, the Son, and the Holy Ghost. Amen."

If you wish to set the thief free, you must tell him to leave in the name of St. John.

(134.) Another Way to Spell-Bind Thieves:

Ye thieves, I conjure you, to be obedient like Jesus Christ, who obeyed his Heavenly Father unto the cross, and to stand without moving out of my sight, in the name of the Trinity. I command you by the power of God and the incarnation of Jesus Christ, not to move out of my sight, + + + like Jesus Christ was standing on Jordan's stormy banks to be baptized by John. And furthermore, I conjure you, horse and rider, to stand still and not to move out of my sight, like Jesus Christ did stand when he was about to be nailed to the cross to release the fathers of the church from the bonds of hell. Ye thieves, I bind you with the same bonds with which Jesus our Lord has bound hell; and thus ye shall be bound; + + + and the same words that bind you shall also release you.

(135.) **To Effect the Same in Less Time:**

Thou horseman and footman, you are coming under your hats; you are scattered! With the blood of Jesus Christ, with his five holy wounds, thy barrel, thy gun, and thy pistol are bound; sabre, sword, and knife are enchanted and bound, in the name of God the Father, the Son, and the Holy Ghost. Amen.

This must be spoken three times.

(136.) **To Release Spell-Bound Persons:**

You horsemen and footmen, whom I here conjured at this time, you may pass on in the name of Jesus Christ, through the word of God and the will of Christ; ride ye on now and pass.

(137.) **To Compel A Thief to Return Stolen Goods.**

Early in the morning before sunrise you must go to a pear tree, and take with you three nails out of a coffin, or three horse-shoe nails that were never used, and holding these toward the rising sun, you must say:

"Oh, thief, I bind you by the first nail, which I drive into thy skull and thy brain, to return the goods thou hast stolen to their former place; thou shalt feel as sick and as anxious to see men, and to see the place you stole from, as felt the disciple Judas after betraying Jesus. I bind thee by the other nail, which I drive into your lungs and liver, to return the stolen goods to their former place; thou shall feel as sick and as anxious to see men, and to see the place you have stolen from, as did Pilate in the fires of hell. The third nail I shall drive into thy foot, oh thief, in order that thou shalt return the stolen goods to the very same place from which thou hast stolen them. Oh, thief, I bind thee and compel thee, by the three holy nails which were driven through the hands and feet of Jesus Christ, to return the stolen goods to the very same place from which thou hast stolen them." + + +

The three nails, however, must be greased with the grease from an executed criminal or other sinful person.

(138.) A Benediction For All Purposes:

Jesus, I will arise; Jesus, do thou accompany me; Jesus, do thou lock my heart into thine, and let my body and my soul be commended unto thee. The Lord is crucified. May God guard my senses that evil spirits may not overcome me, in the name of God the Father, Son, and the Holy Ghost. Amen.

(139.) To Win Every Game One Engages In.

Tie the heart of a bat with a red silken string to the right arm, and you will win every game at cards you play.

(140.) Against Burns:

Our dear Lord Jesus Christ going on a journey, saw a firebrand burning; it was Saint Lorenzo stretched out on a roast. He rendered him assistance and consolation; he lifted his divine hand and blessed the brand; he stopped it from spreading deeper and wider. Thus may the burning be blessed in the name of God the Father, Son and Holy Ghost. Amen.

(141.) Another Remedy for Burns:

Clear out, brand, but never in; be thou cold or hot, thou must cease to burn. May God guard thy blood and thy flesh, thy marrow and thy bones, and every artery, great or small. They all shall be guarded and protected in the name of God against inflammation and mortification, in the name of God the Father, the Son, and the Holy Ghost. Amen.

(142.) To Be Given To Cattle Against Witchcraft.

S A T O R
A R E P O
T E N E T
O P E R A
R O T A S

This must be written on paper and the cattle made to swallow it in their feed.

(143.) How to Tie Up and Heal Wounds.

Speak the following:

"This wound I tie up in three names, in order that thou mayest take from it heat, water, falling off of the flesh, swelling, and all that may be injurious about the swelling, in the name of the Holy Trinity."

This must be spoken three times; then draw a string three times around the wound, and put it under the corner of the house toward the East, and say:

"I put thee there, + + + in order that thou mayest take unto thyself the gathered water, the swelling, and the running, and all that may be injurious about the wound. Amen."

Then repeat the Lord's Prayer and some good hymn.

(144.) To Take the Pain Out of A Fresh Wound:

Our dear Lord Jesus Christ had a great many biles and wounds, and yet he never had them dressed. They did not grow old, they were not cut, nor were they ever found running. Jonas was blind, and I spoke to the heavenly child, as true as five holy wounds were inflicted.

(145.) A Benediction Against Worms:

Peter and Jesus went out upon the fields; they ploughed three furrows, and ploughed up three worms. The one was white, the other was black, and the third one was red. Now all the worms are dead, in the name. + + +

Repeat these words three times.

(146.) Against Every Evil Influence:

Lord Jesus, thy wounds so red will guard me against death.

(147.) To Retain The Right in Court and Council.

Jesus Nazarenus, Rex Judeorum

First carry these characters with you, written on paper, and then repeat the following words:

"I (name) appear before the house of the Judge. Three dead men look out of the window; one having no tongue, the other having no lungs, and the third was sick, blind and dumb."

This is intended to be used when you are standing before a court in your right, and the judge not being favorably disposed toward you. While on your way to the court you must repeat the benediction already given above.

(148.) To Stop Bleeding At Any Time.

Write the name of the four principal waters of the whole world, flowing out of Paradise, on a paper, namely: **Pison, Gihon, Hedekiel and Pheat**, and put it on the wound. In the first book of Moses, the second chapter, verses 11, 12, 13, you will find them. You will find this effective.

(149.) Another Way to Stop Blood.

As soon as you cut yourself you must say: *"Blessed wound, blessed hour, blessed be the day on which Jesus Christ was born, in the name + + + Amen."*

(150.) Another Similar Prescription.

Breathe three times upon the patient, and say the Lord's Prayer three times until the words, *"upon the earth,"* and the bleeding will be stopped.

(151.) Another Still More Certain Way to Stop Bleeding.

If the bleeding will not stop, or if a vein has been cut, then lay the following on it, and it will stop that hour. Yet if any one does not believe this, let him write the letters upon a knife and stab an irrational animal, and he will not be able to draw blood. And whosoever carries this about him will be safe against all his enemies.

*I. m. I. K. I. B. I. P. a. x. v. ss. Ss. vas,
I. P. O. unay Lit. Dom. mper vobism.*

And whenever a woman is going to give birth to a child, or is otherwise afflicted, let her have this letter about her person; it will certainly be of avail.

(152.) A Peculiar Sign to Keep Back Men and Animals.

Whenever you are in danger of being attacked, then carry this sign with you:

"In the name of God, I make the attack. May it please my Redeemer to assist me. Upon the holy assistance of God I depend entirely; upon the holy assistance of God and my gun I rely very truly. God alone be with us. Blessed be Jesus."

(153.) **Protection of One's House and Hearth:**

Beneath thy guardianship I am safe against all tempests and all enemies, J. J. J.

These three J's signify Jesus three times.

(154.) **A Charm to Be Carried About the Person.**

Carry these words about you, and nothing can hit you:

Ananiah, Azariah, and Misael, blessed be the Lord, for he has redeemed us from hell, and has saved us from death, and he has redeemed us out of the fiery furnace, and has preserved us even in the midst of the fire; in the same manner may it please him the Lord that there be no fire.

I.

N. I. R.

I.

(155.) **To Charm Enemies and Murderers:**

God be with you, brethren; stop, ye thieves, robbers, murderers, horsemen, and soldiers, in all humility, for we have tasted the rosy blood of Jesus. Your rifles and guns will be stopped up with the holy blood of Jesus; and all swords and arms are made harmless by the five holy wounds of Jesus. There are three roses upon the heart of God; the first is beneficent, the other is omnipotent, the third is his holy will. You thieves must therefore stand under it, standing still as long as I will. In the name of God the Father, Son and Holy Ghost, you are conjured and made to stand.

(156.) A Charm Against Fire-Arms:

Jesus passed over the Red Sea, and looked upon the land; and thus must break all ropes and bands, and thus must break all manner of fire-arms, rifles, guns, or pistols, and all false tongues be silenced. May the benediction of God on creating the first man always be upon me; the benediction spoken by God, when he ordered in a dream that Joseph and Mary together with Jesus should flee into Egypt, be upon me always, and may the holy + be ever lovely and beloved in my right hand. I journey through the country at large where no one is robbed, killed or murdered — where no one can do me any injury, and where not even a dog could bite me, or any other animal tear me to pieces. In all things let me be protected, as also my flesh and blood, against sins and false tongues which reach from the earth up to heaven, by the power of the four Evangelists, in the name of God the Father, God the Son, and God the Holy Ghost. Amen.

(157.) Another For the Same:

I (name) conjure ye guns, swords and knives, as well as all other kinds of arms, by the spear that pierced the side of God, and opened it so that blood and water could flow out, that ye do not injure me, a servant of God, in the + + +. I conjure ye, by Saint Stephen, who was stoned by the Virgin, that ye cannot injure me who am a servant of God, in the name of + + +. Amen.

(158.) Protection Against All Kinds of Weapons:

Jesus, God and man, do thou protect me against all manner of guns, firearms, long or short, of any kind of metal. Keep thou thy fire, like the Virgin Mary, who kept her fire both before and after her birth. May Christ bind up all fire-arms after the manner of his having bound up himself in humility while in the flesh. Jesus, do thou render harmless all arms and weapons, like unto the husband of Mary the mother of God, he having been harmless likewise. Furthermore, do thou guard the three holy drops of blood which Christ sweated on the Mount of Olives. Jesus Christ! do thou protect me against being killed and against burning fires. Jesus, do thou not suffer me to be killed, much less to be damned, without having received the Lord's Supper. May God the Father, Son, and Holy Ghost, assist me in this. Amen.

(159.) A Charm Against Shooting, Cutting or Thrusting:

In the name of J. J. J. Amen. I (name); Jesus Christ is the true salvation; Jesus Christ governs. reigns, defeats and conquers every enemy, visible or invisible; Jesus, be thou with me at all times, forever and ever, upon all roads and ways, upon the water and the land, on the mountain and in the valley, in the house and in the yard, in the whole world wherever I am, stand, run, ride or drive; there be thou also, Lord Jesus Christ, at all times, late and early, every hour, every moment; and in all my goings in or goings out. Those five holy red wounds, oh, Lord Jesus Christ, may they guard me against all fire-arms, be they secret or public, that they cannot injure me or do me any harm whatever, in the name of + + +. May Jesus Christ, with his guardianship and protection, shield me (name) always from daily commission of sins, worldly injuries and injustice, from contempt, from pestilence and other diseases, from fear, torture, and great suffering, from all evil intentions, from false tongues and old clatter-brains; and that no kind of fire-arms can inflict any injury to my body, do thou take care of me. + + +. And that no band of thieves, highway robbers, incendiaries, witches and other evil spirits may secretly enter my house or premises, nor break in; may the dear Virgin Mary, and all children who are in heaven with God, in eternal joys, protect and guard me against them; and the glory of God the Father shall strengthen me, the wisdom of God the Son shall enlighten me, and the grace of God the Holy Ghost shall empower me from this hour unto all eternity. Amen.

(160.) To Charm Guns and Other Arms:

The blessing which came from heaven at the birth of Christ be with me (name). The blessing of God at the creation of the first man be with me; the blessing of Christ on being imprisoned, bound, lashed, crowned so dreadfully, and beaten, and dying on the cross, be with me; the blessing which the Priest spoke over the tender, joyful corpse of our Lord Jesus Christ, be with me; the constancy of the Holy Mary and all the saints of God, of the three holy kings, Caspar, Melchior and Balthasar, be with me; the holy four Evangelists, Matthew, Mark, Luke and John, be with me; the Archangels St. Michael, St. Gabriel, St. Raphael and St. Uriel, be with me; the twelve holy messengers of the Patriarchs and all the Hosts of Heaven, be with me; and the inexpressible number of all the Saints be with me. Amen.

Papa, R. tarn, Tetregammate Angen.
Jesus Nazarenus, Rex Judeorum.

(161.) **To Prevent Being Cheated, Charmed or Bewitched, and to Be at All Times Blessed:**

Like unto the cup and the wine, and the holy supper, which our dear Lord Jesus Christ gave unto his dear disciples on Maunday Thursday, may the Lord Jesus guard me in daytime, and at night, that no dog may bite me, no wild beast tear me to pieces, no tree fall on me, no water rise against me, no fire-arms injure me, no weapons, no steel, no iron, cut me, no fire burn me, no false sentence fall upon me, no false tongue injure me, no rogue enrage me, and that no fiends, no witchcraft and enchantment can harm me. Amen.

(162.) Different Directions to Effect the Same:

The Holy Trinity guard me, and be and remain with me on the water and upon the land, in the water or in the fields, in cities or villages, in the whole world wherever I am. The Lord Jesus Christ protect me against all my enemies, secret or public; and may the Eternal Godhead also guard me through the bitter sufferings of Jesus Christ; his holy rosy blood, shed on the cross, assist me, J. J. Jesus has been crucified, tortured and died. These are true words, and in the same way must all words be efficacious which are here put down, and spoken in prayer by me. This shall assist me that I shall not be imprisoned, bound or overcome by anyone. Before me all guns or other weapons shall be of no use or power. Fire-arms, hold your fire in the almighty hand of God. This all fire-arms shall be charmed. + + + When the right hand of the Lord Jesus Christ was fastened to the tree of the cross; like unto the Son of the Heavenly Father who was obedient unto death, may the Eternal Godhead protect me by the rosy blood, by the five holy wounds on the tree of the cross; and thus must I be blessed and well protected like the cup and the wine, and the genuine true bread, which Jesus Christ gave to his disciples on the evening of Maunday Thursday. J. J. J.

(163.) Another Similar Direction:

The grace of God and his benevolence be with me (N). I shall now ride or walk out; and I will gird about my loins with a sure ring. So it pleases God, the Heavenly Father, he will protect me, my flesh and blood, and all my arteries and limbs, during this day and night *which I have before me; and however numerous my enemies might be, they must be dumbstruck, and all become like a dead man, white as snow, so that no one will be able to shoot, cut or throw at me, or to overcome me, although he may hold rifle or steel against whosoever else evil weapons and arms might be called, in his hand. My rifle shall go off like the lightning from heaven, and my sword shall cut like a razor. Then went our dear lady Mary upon a very high mountain; she looked down into a very dusky valley and beheld her dear child standing amidst the Jews, harsh, very harsh, because he was bound so harsh, because he was bound so hard; and therefore may the dear Lord Jesus Christ save me from all that is injurious to me. + + + Amen.*

(164.) Another Similar Direction:

There walk out during this day and night, that thou mayest not let any of my enemies, or thieves, approach me, if they do not intend to bring me what was spent from the holy altar. Because God the Lord Jesus Christ is ascended into heaven in his living body. O Lord, this is good for me this day and night. + + + Amen.

(165.) Another One Like It:

In the name of God I walk out. God the Father be with me, and God the Holy Ghost be by my side. Whoever is stronger than these three persons may approach my body and my life; yet whoso is not stronger than these three would much better let me be. J. J. J.

(166.) Another One Like It:

I conjure thee, sword, sabre or knife, that mightest injure or harm me, by the priest of all prayers, who had gone into the temple at Jerusalem, and said: An edged sword shall pierce your soul that you may not injure me, who am a child of God.

(167.) **A Very Effective Charm:**

I (name) conjure thee, sword or knife, as well as all other weapons, by that spear which pierced Jesus' side, and opened it to the gushing out of blood and water, that he keep me from injury as one of the servants of God. + + + Amen.

(168.) **A Very Safe and Reliable Charm:**

The peace of our Lord Jesus Christ be with me [name]. Oh shot, stand still! in the name of the mighty prophets Agtion and Elias, and do not kill me! oh shot, stop short. I conjure you by heaven and earth, and by the last judgment, that you do no harm unto me, a child of God. + + +

(169.) **A Good Charm Against Thieves:**

There are three lilies standing upon the grave of the Lord our God; the first one is the courage of God, the other is the blood of God, and the third one is the will of God. Stand still, thief! No more than Jesus Christ stepped down from the cross, no more shalt thou move from this spot; this I command thee by the four evangelists and elements of heaven, there in the river, or in the shot, or in the judgment, or in the sight. Thus I conjure you by the last judgment to stand still and not to move, until I see all the stars in heaven and the sun rises again. Thus I stop by running and jumping and command it in the name of + + +. Amen.

This must be repeated three times.

(170.) **How to Recover Stolen Goods.**

Take good care to notice through which door the thief passed out, and cut off three small chips from the posts of that door; then take these three chips to a wagon, unbeshrewdly, however; take off one of the wheels and put the three chips into the stock of the wheel, in the three highest names, then turn the wheel backwards and say:

Thief, thief, thief! Turn back with the stolen goods; thou art forced to do it by the Almighty power of God: + + + God the Father calls thee back, God the Son turns thee back so that thou must return, and God the Holy Ghost leads thee back, until thou arrive at the place from which thou hast stolen. By the almighty power of God the Father thou must come; by the wisdom of God the Son thou hast neither peace nor quiet until thou hast returned the stolen goods to their former place; by the grace of God the Holy Ghost thou must run and jump and canst find no peace or rest until thou arrivest at the place from which thou hast stolen. God the Father binds thee, God the Son forces thee, and God the Holy Ghost turns thee back. (You must not turn the wheel too fast.) Thief, thou must come, + + + thief, thou must come, + + + thief, thou must come, + + +. If thou art more almighty, thief, thief, thief; if thou art more almighty than God himself, then you may remain where you are. The Ten Commandments force thee — thou shalt not steal, and therefore thou must come. + + + Amen.

(171.) A Well-Tried Charm:

Three holy drops of blood have passed down the holy cheeks of the Lord God, and these three holy drops of blood are placed before the touchhole. As surely as our dear lady was pure from all men, as surely shall no fire or smoke pass out of this barrel. Barrel, do thou give neither fire, nor flame, nor heat. Now I will walk out, because the Lord God goeth before me; God the Son is with me, and God the Holy Ghost is about me forever.

(172.) Another Well-Tried Charm Against Fire-Arms.

Blessed is the hour in which Jesus Christ was born; blessed is the hour in which Jesus Christ was born; blessed is the hour in which Jesus Christ was born; blessed is the hour in which Jesus Christ has arisen from the dead; blessed are these three hours over thy gun, that no shot or ball shall fly toward me, and neither my skin, nor my hair, nor my blood, nor my flesh be injured by them, and that no kind of weapon or metal shall do me any harm, so surely as the Mother of God shall not bring forth another son. + + +. Amen.

(173.) A Charm to Gain Advantage of a Man of Superior Strength:

I [name] breathe upon thee. Three drops of blood I take from thee: the first out of thy heart, the other out of thy liver, and the third out of thy vital powers: and in this I deprive thee of thy strength and manliness.

Hbbi Massa danti Lantien. I. I. I.

(174.) A Recipe for Destroying Spring-Tails or Ground-Fleas.

Take the chaff upon which children have been lying in their cradles, or take the dung of horses, and put that upon the field, and the spring-tails or ground-fleas will no longer do you any injury.

(175.) A Benediction for and Against all Enemies:

The cross of Christ be with me; the cross of Christ overcomes all water and every fire; the cross of Christ overcomes all weapons; the cross of Christ is a perfect sign and blessing to my soul. May

Christ be with me and my body during all my life at day and at night. Now I pray, I, [name], pray God the Father for the soul's sake, and I pray God the Son for the Father's sake, and I pray God the Holy Ghost for the Father's and the Son's sake, that the holy corpse of God may bless me against all evil things, words and works. The cross of Christ open unto me future bliss; the cross of Christ be with me, above me, before me, behind me, beneath me, aside of me and everywhere, and before all my enemies, visible and invisible; these all flee from me as soon as they but know or hear. Enoch and Elias, the two prophets, were never imprisoned, nor bound, nor beaten and came never out of their power; thus no one of my enemies must be able to injure or attack me in my body or my life, in the name of God the Father, the Son, and the Holy Ghost. Amen.

(176.) **A Benediction Against Enemies, Sickness and Misfortune:**

The blessing which came from heaven, from God the Father, when the true living Son was born, be with me at all times; the blessing which God spoke over the whole human race, be with me always. The holy cross of God, as long and as broad as the one upon which God suffered his blessed, bitter tortures, bless me to-day and forever. The three holy nails which were driven through the holy hands and feet of Jesus Christ shall bless me to-day and forever. The bitter crown of thorns which was forced upon the holy head of Christ, shall bless me to-day and forever. The spear by which the holy side of Jesus was opened, shall bless me to-day and forever. The rosy blood protects me from all my enemies, and from everything which might be injurious to my body or soul, or my worldly goods. Bless me, oh ye five holy wounds, in order that all my enemies may be driven away and bound, while God has encompassed all Christendom. In this shall assist me God the Father, the Son and the Holy Ghost. Amen. Thus must I [name] be blessed as well and as valid as the cup and the wine, and the true, living bread which Jesus gave his disciples on the evening of Maunday Thursday. All those that hate you must be silent before me; their hearts are dead in regard to me; and their tongues are mute, so that they are not at all able to inflict the least injury upon me, or my house, or my premises: And likewise, all those who intend attacking and wounding me with their arms and weapons shall be defenceless, weak and conquered before me. In this shall assist me the holy power of God, which can make all arms or weapons of no avail. All this in the name of God the Father, the Son, and the Holy Ghost. Amen.

(177.) **The Talisman.**

It is said that anyone going out hunting and carrying it in his game-bag, cannot but shoot something worth while and bring it home.

An old hermit once found an old, lame huntsman in a forest, lying beside the road and weeping. The hermit asked him the cause of his dejection. "Ah me, thou man of God, I am a poor, unfortunate being; I must annually furnish my lord with as many deer, and hares, and partridges, as a young and healthy huntsman could hunt up, or else I will be discharged from my office; now I am old and lame; besides game is getting scarce, and I cannot follow it up as I ought to; and I know not what will become of me." Here the old man's feelings overcame him, and he could not utter another word.

The hermit, upon this, took out a small piece of paper, upon which he wrote some words with a pencil, and handing it to the huntsman, he said: "there, old friend, put this in your game-bag whenever you go out hunting, and you shall certainly shoot something worth while, and bring it home, too; yet be careful to shoot no more than you necessarily need, nor to communicate it to anyone that might misuse it, on account of the high meaning contained in these words."

The hermit then went on his journey, and after a little the huntsman also arose, and without thinking of anything in particular he went into the woods, and had scarcely advanced a hundred yards when he shot as fine a roebuck as he ever saw in his life. This huntsman was afterward and during his whole lifetime lucky in his hunting, so much so that he was considered one of the best hunters in that whole country. The following is what the hermit wrote on the paper:

Ut nemo in sense tentat, descendre nemo.

At precedenti spectatur mantica tergo.

The best argument is to try it.

(178.) To Prevent Anyone From Killing Game:

Pronounce the name, as for instance, Jacob Wohlgemuth, shoot whatever you please; shoot but hair and feathers with and what you give to poor people. + + + Amen.

(179.) To Compel A Thief to Return Stolen Goods.

Walk out early in the morning before sunrise, to a juniper-tree, and bend it with the left hand toward the rising sun, while you are saying:

"Juniper-tree, I shall bend and squeeze thee, until the thief has returned the stolen goods to the place from which he took them."

Then you must take a stone and put it on the bush, and under the bush and the stone you must place the skull of a malefactor. + + +

Yet you must be careful, in case the thief returns the stolen goods, to unloose the bush and replace the stone where it was before.

(180.) A Charm Against Powder and Ball:

The heavenly and holy trumpet blow every ball and misfortune away from me. I seek refuge beneath the tree of life which bears twelvefold fruits. I stand behind the holy altar of the Christian

Church. I commend myself to the Holy Trinity. I [name] hide myself beneath the holy corpse of Jesus Christ. I commend myself unto the wounds of Jesus Christ, that the hand of no man might be able to seize me, or to bind me, or to cut me, or to throw me, or to beat me, or to overcome me in any way what ever, so help me. [name]

Whoever carries this book with him is safe from all his enemies, visible or invisible; and whoever has this book with him cannot die without the holy corpse of Jesus Christ, nor drown in any water, nor burn up in any fire, nor can any unjust sentence be passed upon him. So help me. + + +

(181.) Unlucky Days, To Be Found in Each Month.

January 1, 2, 3, 4, 6, 11, 12.
February 1, 17, 18.
March 14, 16.
April 10, 17, 18.
May 7, 8.
June 17.
July 17, 21.
August 20, 21.
September 10, 18.
October 6.
November 6, 10.
December 6, 11, 15.

Whoever is born upon one of these days is unfortunate and suffers much poverty; and whoever takes sick on one of these days seldom recovers health; and those who engage or marry on these days become very poor and miserable. Neither is it advisable to move from one house to another, nor to travel, nor to bargain, nor to engage in a lawsuit, on one of these days. The Signs of the Zodiac must be observed by the course of the moon, as they are daily given in common almanacs. If a cow calves in the sign of the Virgin, the calf will not live one year; if it happens in the Scorpion, it will die much sooner; therefore no one should be weaned off in these signs, nor in the sign of the Capricorn or Aquarius, and they will be in less danger from mortal inflammation. This is the only piece extracted from a centennial almanac imported from Germany, and there are many who believe in it. **HOHMAN.**

(182.) IN CONCLUSION THE FOLLOWING MORNING PRAYER IS GIVEN, WHICH IS TO BE SPOKEN BEFORE ENTERING UPON A JOURNEY. IT PROTECTS AGAINST ALL MANNER OF BAD LUCK.

Oh, Jesus of Nazareth, King of the Jews, yea, a King over the whole world, protect me [name] during this day and night, protect me at all times by thy five holy wounds, that I may not be seized and bound. The Holy Trinity guard me, that no gun, fire-arm, ball or lead, shall touch my body; and that they shall be weak like the tears and bloody sweat of Jesus Christ, in the name of God the Father, the Son and the Holy Ghost. Amen.

APPENDIX

{183.} The following remedy for Epilepsy was published in Lancaster (Pa.) papers, in the year 1828.

TO SUFFERING HUMANITY

We ourselves know of many unfortunate beings who are afflicted with epilepsy, yet how many more may be in the country who have perhaps already spent their fortunes in seeking aid in this disease, without gaining relief. We have now been informed of a remedy which is said to be infallible, and which has been adopted by the most distinguished physicians in Europe, and has so well stood the test of repeated trials that it is now generally applied in Europe.

It directs a bedroom for the sick person to be fitted up over the cow-stable, where the patient must sleep at night, and should spend the greater part of his time during the day in it. This is easily done by building a regular room over the stable.

Then care is to be taken to leave an opening in the ceiling of the stable, in such a manner that the evaporation from the same can pass into the room, while, at the same time, the cow may inhale the perspiration of the sick person. In this way the animal will gradually attract the whole disease, and be affected with arthritic attacks, and when the patient has entirely lost them the cow will fall dead to the ground. The stable must not be cleaned during the operation, though fresh straw or hay may be put in; and of course, the milk of the cow, so long as she gives any, must be thrown away as useless.

[Lancaster Eagle]

{184.} A SALVE TO HEAL UP WOUNDS

Take tobacco, green or dry; if green a good handful, if dry, two ounces; together with this take a good handful of elder leaves, fry them well in butter, press it through a cloth, and you may use it in a salve. This will heal up a wound in a short time.

Or go to a white oak tree that stands pretty well isolated, and scrape off the rough bark from the eastern side of the tree; then cut off the inner bark, break it into small pieces, and boil it until all the strength is drawn out; strain it through a piece of linen, and boil it again, until it becomes as thick as tar; then take out as much as you need, and put to it an equal proportion of sheep-tallow, rosin and wax, and work them together until they form a salve. This salve you put on a piece of linen, very thinly spread, and lay it on the wound, renewing it occasionally till the wound is healed up.

Or take a handful of parsley, pound it fine, and work it to a salve with an equal proportion of fresh butter. This salve prevents mortification and heals very fast.

{185.} PEACHES

The flowers of the peach-tree, prepared like salad, opens the bowels, and is of use in the dropsy. Six or seven peeled kernels of the peach-stone, eaten daily, will ease the gravel; they are also said to prevent drunkenness, when eaten before meals. Whoever loses his hair should pound up peach kernels, mix them with vinegar, and put them on the bald place. The water distilled from peach flowers opens the bowels of infants and destroys their worms.

{186.} SWEET OIL

Sweet oil possesses a great many valuable properties, and it is therefore advisable for every head of a family to have it at all times about the house in order that it may be applied in cases of necessity. Here follow some of its chief virtues:

It is a sure remedy, internally as well as externally, in all cases of inflammation in men and animals. Internally, it is given to allay the burning in the stomach caused by strong drink or by purging too severely, or by poisonous medicines. Even if pure poison has been swallowed, vomiting may be easily produced by one or two wine-glasses of sweet oil, and thus the poison will be carried off, provided it has not already been too long in the bowels; and after the vomiting, a spoonful of the oil should be taken every hour until the burning caused by the poison is entirely allayed.

Whoever is bitten by a snake, or any other poisonous animal, or by a mad dog, and immediately takes warmed sweet oil, and washes the wound with it, and then puts a rag, three or four times doubled up and well soaked with oil, on the wound every three or four hours, and drinks a couple of spoonfuls of the oil every four hours for some days, will surely find out what peculiar virtues the sweet oil possesses in regard to poisons.

In dysentery, sweet oil is likewise a very useful remedy, when the stomach has first been cleansed with rhubarb or some other suitable purgative, and then a few spoonfuls of sweet oil should be taken every three hours. For this purpose, however, the sweet oil should have been well boiled and a little hartshorn be mixed with it. This boiled sweet oil is also serviceable in all sorts of bowel complaints and in colics; or when anyone receives internal injury as from a fall, a few spoonfuls of it should be taken every two hours; for it allays the pain, scatters the coagulated blood, prevents all inflammation and heals gently. Externally, it is applicable in all manner of swellings; it softens, allays the pain, and prevents inflammation.

Sweet oil and white lead, ground together, makes a very good salve, which is applicable in burns and scalds. This salve is also excellent against infection from poisonous weeds or waters, if it is put on the infected part as soon as it is noticed.

If sweet oil is put in a large glass, so as to fill it about one-half full, and the glass in then filled up with the flowers of the St. Johnswort, and well covered and placed in the sun for about four weeks, the oil proves then, when distilled, such a valuable remedy for all fresh wounds in men and animals, that no one can imagine its medicinal powers who has not tried it. This should at all times be found in a well-conducted household. In a similar manner, an oil may be made of white lilies, which is likewise very useful to soften hardened swellings and burns, and to cure the sore breasts of women.

{187.} CURE FOR DROPSY

Dropsy is a disease derived from a cold humidity, which passes through the different limbs to such a degree that it either swells the whole or a portion of them. The usual symptoms and precursors of every case of dropsy are the swelling of the feet and thighs, and then of the face; besides this the change of the natural color of the flesh into a dull white, with great thirst, loss of appetite, costiveness, sweating, throwing up of slimy substances, but little water, laziness and aversion to exercise.

Physicians know three different kinds of dropsy, which they name:

1. Anasarca, when the water penetrates between the skin and the flesh over the whole body, and all the limbs, and even about the face and swells them.

2. Ascites, when the belly and thighs swell, while the upper extremities dry up.

3. Tympanites, caused rather by wind than water. The belly swells up very hard, the navel is forced out very far, and the other members fall away. The belly becomes so much inflated that knocking against it causes a sound like that of a large drum, and from this circumstance its name is derived.

The chief thing in curing dropsy rests upon three points, namely:

1. To reduce the hardness of the swelling which may be in the

bowels or other parts.

2. To endeavor to scatter the humors.

3. To endeavor to pass them off either through the stool or through the water.

The best cure therefore must chiefly consist in this: To avoid as much as possible all drinking and use only dry victuals; to take moderate exercise, and to sweat and purge the body considerably.

If anyone feels symptoms of dropsy, or while it is yet in its first stages, let him make free use of the sugar of the herb called Fumatory, as this purifies the blood, and the Euphrasy sugar to open the bowels.

{188.} A CURE FOR DROPSY (SAID TO BE INFALLIBLE)

Take a jug of stone or earthenware, and put four quarts of strong, healthy cider into it; take two handfuls of parsley roots and tops, cut it fine; a handful of scraped horse-radish, two tablespoonfuls of bruised mustard-seed, half an ounce of squills, and half an ounce of juniper berries; put all these in the jug, and place it near the fire for 24 hours so as to keep the cider warm, and shake it up often; then strain it through a cloth and keep it for use.

To a grown person give half a wineglassful three times a day, on an empty stomach. But if necessary you may increase the dose, although it must decrease again as soon as the water is carried off, and, as stated before, use dry victuals and exercise gently.

This remedy has cured a great many persons, and among them a woman of 70 years of age, who had the dropsy so badly that she was afraid to get out of bed, for fear her skin might burst, and who it was thought could not live but a few days. She used this remedy according to the directions given, and in less than a week the water had passed off her, the swelling of her stomach fell, and in a few weeks afterward she again enjoyed perfect health.

Or: Drink for a few days very strong Bohea tea, and eat the leaves of it. This simple means is said to have carried away the water from some persons in three or four days, and freed them from the swelling, although this disease had reached the highest pitch.

Or: Take three spoonfuls of rape-seed, and half an ounce of clean gum myrrh, put these together in a quart of good old wine, and let it stand over night in the room, keeping it well covered. Aged persons are to take two teaspoonfuls of this an hour after supper, and the same before going to bed; younger persons must diminish the quantity according to their age, and continue the use of it as long as necessary.

Or: Take young branches of spruce pine, cut them into small pieces, pour water on them and let them boil a while, then pour it into a large tub, take off your clothes, and sit down over it, covering yourself and the tub with a sheet or blanket, to prevent the vapor from escaping. When the water begins to cool let some one put in hot bricks; and when you have thus been sweating for a while, wrap the sheet or blanket close around you and go to bed with it. A repetition of this for several days will free the system from all water.

The following Valuable Recipes, not in the original work of Hohman, are added by the publisher.

{189.} CURE FOR DROPSY

Take of the broom-corn seed, well powdered and sifted, one drachm. Let it steep twelve hours in a wineglass and a half of good, rich wine, and take it in the morning fasting, having first shaken it so that the whole may be swallowed. Let the patient walk after it, if able, or let him use what exercise he can without fatigue, for an hour and a half; after which let him take two ounces of olive oil, and not eat or drink anything in less than half an hour afterward. Let this be repeated every day, or once in three days, and not oftener, till a cure is effected, and do not let blood, or use any other remedy during the course.

Nothing can be more gentle and safe than the operation of this remedy. If the dropsy is in the body it discharges it by water, without any inconvenience; if it is between the skin and flesh, it cases blisters to rise on the legs, by which it will run off; but this does not happen to more than one in thirty: and in this case no plasters must be used, but apply red-cabbage leaves. It cures dropsy in pregnant women, without injury to the mother or child. It also alleviates asthma, consumption and disorders of the liver.

{190.} REMEDY FOR THE LOCK JAW

We are informed by a friend that a sure preventive against this terrible disease, is, to take some soft soap and mix it with a sufficient quantity of pulverized chalk, so as to make it of the consistency of buckwheat batter; keep the chalk moistened with a fresh supply of soap until the wound begins to discharge, and the patient finds relief. Our friend stated to us that explicit confidence may be placed in what he says, that he has known several cases where this remedy has been successfully applied. So simple and valuable a remedy, within the reach of everyone, ought to be generally known. —

N.Y. Evening Post

{191.} FOR THE STING OF A WASP OR BEE

A Liverpool paper states as follows: "A few days ago, happening to be in the country, we witnessed the efficacy of the remedy for the sting of a wasp mentioned in one of our late papers. A little boy was stung severely and was in great torture, until an onion was applied to the part affected, when the cure was instantaneous. This important and simple remedy cannot be too generally known, and we pledge ourselves to the facts above stated."

{192.} DIARRHEA MIXTURE

Take one ounce tincture of rhubarb, one ounce laudanum, one ounce tincture of Cayenne pepper, and one ounce spirits of camphor. Dose is from ten to thirty drops for an adult.

{193.} SOAP POWDERS

Take one pound of hard soap, cut it fine, and mix with it one pound of soda ash. This preparation, we believe, is a "great secret."

{194.} TO DYE A MADDER RED

For each pound of cloth, soak half a pound of madder in a brass kettle over night, with sufficient warm water to cover the cloth you intend to dye. Next morning put in two ounces of madder compound for every pound of madder. Wet your cloth and wring it out in clean water, then put it into the dye. Place the kettle over the fire, and bring it slowly to a scalding heat, which will take about half an hour; keep at this heat half an hour, if a light red is wanted, and longer if a dark one, the color depending on the time it remains in the dye. When you have obtained the color, rinse the cloth immediately in cold water.

{195.} TO DYE A FINE SCARLET RED

Bring to a boiling heat, in a brass kettle, sufficient soft water to cover the cloth you wish to dye; then add 1 1/2 oz. cream of tartar for every pound of cloth. Boil a minute or two, add two oz. lac dye and one oz. madder compound (both previously mixed in an earthen bowl), boil five minutes; now wet the cloth in warm water and wring it out and put in into the dye; boil the whole nearly an hour, take the cloth out and rinse it in clear cold water.

{196.} TO DYE A PERMANENT BLUE

Boil the cloth in a brass kettle for an hour, in a solution containing fire parts of alum and three of tartar for every 32 parts of cloth. It is then to be thrown into warm water, previously mixed with a greater or less proportion of chemic blue, according to the shade the cloth is intended to receive. In this water it must be boiled until it has acquired the desired color.

{197.} TO DYE A GREEN

For every pound of cloth add 3 1/2 oz. of alum and one pound of fustic. Steep (not boil) till the strength is out; soak the cloth till it acquires a good yellow, then remove the chips, and add the chemic blue by degrees till you have the desired color.

{198.} PHYSIC BALL FOR HORSES

Cape aloes, from six to ten drachms; Castile soap, one drachm; spirits of wine, one drachm; syrup to form the ball. If mercurial physic be wanted, add from one-half a drachm to one drachm of calomel.

Previous to physicking a horse, and during its operation, he should be fed on bran mashes, allowed plenty of chilled water, and have exercise. Physic is always useful; it is necessary to be administered in almost every disease; it improves digestion, and gives strength to the lacteals by cleansing the intestines and unloading the liver; and if the animal is afterward properly fed, will improve his strength and condition in a remarkable degree. Physic, except in urgent cases, should be given in the morning and on an empty stomach, and, if required to be repeated, a week should intervene between each dose.

Before giving a horse a ball, see that it is not too hard nor too large. Cattle medicine is always given as a drench.

{199.} PHYSIC FOR CATTLE

Cape aloes, four drachms to one oz.; Epsom salts, four to six oz.; powdered ginger, three drachms. Mix and give in a quart of gruel. For calves, one-third of this will be a dose.

{200.} SEDATIVE AND WORM BALL

Powdered white hellebore, one-half drachm; linseed powder, one-half oz. If necessary, make into a ball with molasses. This ball is a specific for weed. Two ounces of gargling oil, in one-half bottle of linseed oil, is an effectual remedy for worms in horses and cattle.

{201.} ASTRINGENT BALL FOR LOOSENESS IN HORSES

Opium from one-half to one drachm; ginger, one and a half drachms; prepared chalk, three drachms; flour, two drachms. Powder, and make into a ball with molasses.

{202.} MIXTURE FOR ULCERS AND ALL FOUL SORES

Sulphate of zinc, one oz.; corrosive sublimate, one drachm; spirit of salt, four drachms; water, one pint; mix.

{203.} YELLOW WATER IN HORSES

Take Venetian soap, juniper oil, saltpetre, sal prunella, sweet spirits of nitre, of each one ounce; make it into a ball with pulverized licorice root, and give the horse two ounces at once, and repeat if necessary. If attended with a violent fever, bleed, and give bran mashes; or, take a gallon of strong beer, or ale, add thereto two ounces of Castile soap and one ounce of saltpetre; stir, and mix daily of this with his feed. The following is also highly recommended in a German work: Take pulverized gentian and calamus, of each one-half ounce; sulphate of potassa, two ounces; tartar emetic, liver of sulphur, and oil of turpentine, one-eighth of an ounce each; mix it with flour and water, and give the above in the incipient stage of the disease. The dose, if necessary, may be given daily for several days.

{204.} A VALUABLE RECIPE FOR GALLS — WINDGALLS IN HORSES.

An intelligent and experienced farmer, rising of seventy years of age, residing in Allen Township, Cumberland County, has assured us that the following ointment, if applied two or three times a day, will cure the most obstinate windgalls.

Take one pound of the leaves of stramonium (Jamestown weed) bruised; two pounds of fresh butter or hog's lard, and one gill of the spirits of turpentine; put the whole of the ingredients into a clean earthen crock and place it with the contents over live coals for twenty or thirty minutes, stirring it occasionally: then strain it through a coarse cloth or canvas, and it forms a consistent ointment, with which anoint the windgalls two or three times a day.

Fifty dollars had been offered for the above recipe, so says our informant, who kindly furnished it.

{205.} WIND-BROKEN HORSES

The excellent ball for broken-winded horses that has made a perfect cure of over seven hundred in less than nine months, after many other medicines being tried in vain. Take myrrh, elecampane, and licorice root, in fine powder, three ounces each; saffron, three drachms: assafoetida, one ounce; sulphur squills and cinnabar of antimony, of each two ounces; aurum mosaicum, one ounce and a half; oil of aniseed, eighty drops. You may make it into paste with either treacle or honey, and give the horse the quantity of a hen's egg every morning for a week; and afterwards every other morning till the disorder is removed. — [*Montague's Farrier*, page 57.]

Gypsy Witch Book of Old Pennsylvania Dutch Pow-Wows and Hexes

INDEX TO THE ARTS AND REMEDIES CONTAINED IN THIS BOOK

ARTS AND REMEDIES

{001.} A good remedy for hysterics.
{002.} Another remedy for hysterics.
{003.} A certain remedy to stop bleeding.
{004.} A remedy to prevent failing away.
{005.} Another remedy to be applied when anyone is sick.
{006.} A good remedy for worms.
{007.} A good remedy against slander.
{008.} A good remedy for the colic.
{009.} A good remedy for the fever.
{010.} To attach a dog to a person.
{011.} A very good remedy for palpitation of the heart.
{012.} A precaution against injuries.
{013.} To make a wand for searching for iron or water.
{014.} How to obtain things desired.
{015.} A sure way of catching fish.
{016.} A safe remedy for various ulcers, ect.
{017.} A good remedy for mortification and inflammation.
{018.} To prevent malicious persons from doing injury.
{019.} To destroy bots or worms in horses.
{020.} To cure the poll-evil in horses, in two or three applications.
{021.} A good remedy for wounds and burns.
{022.} A good remedy for the wild-fire.
{023.} To stop pains or smarting in a wound.
{024.} To destroy warts.
{025.} To banish the whooping cough.
{026.} Another remedy for whopping cough.
{027.} A good way to stop bleeding.
{028.} A good remedy for the toothache.
{029.} How to walk and step securely in all cases.
{030.} A very good remedy for the colic.
{031.} To banish convulsive fevers.
{032.} How to banish the fever.
{033.} A very good plaster.
{034.} To make a good eye-water.

Gypsy Witch Book of Old Pennsylvania Dutch Pow-Wows and Hexes

{035.} Remedy for white swelling.
{036.} Remedy for epilepsy.
{037.} Remedy for burns.
{038.} To stop bleeding.
{039.} Remedy to relieve pain.
{040.} Remedy for the toothache.
{041.} To remove bruises and pains.
{042.} A remarkable passage from the book of Albertus Magnus.
{043.} Another passage from the same.
{044.} To cure fits or convulsions.
{045.} Cure for the headache.
{046.} To mend broken glass.
{047.} To make cattle return to the same place.
{048.} Another method of making cattle return.
{049.} To prevent the Hessian fly from injuring wheat.
{050.} To prevent cherries from ripening before Martinmas.
{051.} Stinging nettles - good for banishing fears and fancies, and to cause fish to collect.
{052.} Heliotrope, a means to prevent calumniation.
{053.} To heal a sore mouth.
{054.} A good remedy for consumption.
{055.} Swallow-Wort: Its properties.
{056.} For the hollow horn in cows.
{057.} To destroy the wheal in the eye.
{058.} To make hens lay many eggs.
{059.} Words to be spoken while making divinatory wands.
{060.} How to destroy a tape-worm.
{061.} A good remedy for the bots in horses.
{062.} How to cure a burn.
{063.} To cure the bite of a snake.
{064.} Security against mad dogs.
{065.} To remove pain and heal wounds with three switches.
{066.} Remedy for fever, worms and the colic.
{067.} How to cure weakness of the limbs.
{068.} Another remedy for weakness.
{069.} To make horses that refuse their feed to eat again.
{070.} A good method of destroying rats and mice.
{071.} To cure any excrescence or wen on a horse.

Gypsy Witch Book of Old Pennsylvania Dutch Pow-Wows and Hexes

{072.} How to prepare a good eye-water.
{073.} How to cause thieves to stand still.
{074.} To cure the sweeney in horses.
{075.} How to make molasses.
{076.} To make good beer.
{077.} Cure for the epilepsy.
{078.} Another way to make cattle return home.
{079.} A very good remedy to cure sores.
{080.} A good cure for wounds.
{081.} To make an oil out of paper, good for sore eyes.
{082.} To destroy crab-lice.
{083.} To prevent the worst kind of paper from blotting.
{084.} A very good remedy for the gravel.
{085.} A good remedy for those who cannot keep their water.
{086.} To remove a wen during the crescent moon.
{087.} To destroy field-mice and moles.
{088.} To remove a scum or skin from the eye.
{089.} For deafness, buzzing in the ear, ect.
{090.} To cause children to cut their teeth without pain.
{091.} For vomiting and diarrhea.
{092.} To heal burns.
{093.} A very good cure for weakness of the limbs, ect.
{094.} For dysentery and diarrhea.
{095.} Cure for the toothache.
{096.} Advice to pregnant women.
{097.} Cure for the bite of a mad dog.
{098.} A very good means to increase the growth of wool on sheep, and to prevent disease among them.
{099.} A well-tried plaster to remove mortification.
{100.} A good remedy for the poll-evil in horses.
{101.} For the scurvy and sore throat.
{102.} A very good plaster.
{103.} To stop bleeding.
{104.} Another way to stop bleeding, and to heal wounds.
{105.} For gaining a lawful suit.
{106.} For the swelling of cattle.
{107.} An easy method of catching fish.
{108.} A very good and safe remedy for the rheumatism.

Gypsy Witch Book of Old Pennsylvania Dutch Pow-Wows and Hexes

{109.} A good way to destroy worms in bee-hives.
{110.} For making a paste to prevent gun-barrels from rusting.
{111.} To make a wick which is never consumed.
{112.} A morning prayer before entering upon a journey.
{113.} A safe and approved means to be applied in time of fire and pestilence.
{114.} To prevent conflagration.
{115.} To prevent witches from bewitching cattle, and against bad men and evil spirits.
{116.} To extinguish fire without water.
{117.} To prevent bad people from getting about the cattle.
{118.} Another method of stopping fire.
{119.} How to fasten or spell-bind anything.
{120.} Another way to spell-bind.
{121.} A benediction to prevent fire.
{122.} How to relieve persons or animals after being bewitched.
{123.} To protect houses and premises against sickness and theft.
{124.} Against mishaps and dangers in the house.
{125.} A direction for a gypsy sentence, ect.
{126.} Against evil spirits and all manner of witchcraft.
{127.} Against swellings.
{128.} How to treat a cow after the milk is taken from her.
{129.} Against adversities, etc.
{130.} Against danger and death.
{131.} Another method of treating a sick cow.
{132.} Against fevers.
{133.} To spell-bind a thief.
{134.} Another way to spell-bind thieves.
{135.} To effect the same in less time.
{136.} To release spell-bound persons.
{137.} To compel a thief to return stolen goods.
{138.} A benediction for all purposes.
{139.} To win every game you engage in at cards.
{140.} Against burns.
{141.} Another remedy for burns.
{142.} To protect cattle against witchcraft.
{143.} How to tie up and heal wounds.
{144.} To take the pain out of fresh wounds.

Gypsy Witch Book of Old Pennsylvania Dutch Pow-Wows and Hexes

{145.} A benediction against worms.
{146.} Against every evil influence.
{147.} To retain the right in a court of justice.
{148.} To stop bleeding at any time.
{149.} Another way to stop blood.
{150.} Another similar prescription.
{151.} Another still more certain way.
{152.} A sign to keep back men and animals.
{153.} Protection to house and hearth.
{154.} A charm, to be carried about the person.
{155.} To charm enemies, robbers and murderers.
{156.} A charm against fire-arms.
{157.} Another for the same.
{158.} Protection against weapons.
{159.} A charm against shooting, ect.
{160.} To charm guns and other arms.
{161.} To prevent being cheated, charmed or bewitched.
{162.} Another to effect the same.
{163.} Another similar direction.
{164.} Another similar direction.
{165.} Another one like it.
{166.} Another one like it.
{167.} A very effective charm.
{168.} A very safe and reliable charm.
{169.} A good charm against thieves.
{170.} How to recover stolen goods.
{171.} A well-tried charm.
{172.} Another against fire-arms.
{173.} A charm to gain advantage over stronger persons.
{174.} To destroy spring-tails or ground fleas.
{175.} A benediction for and against all enemies.
{176.} Another against sickness and misfortune.
{177.} The Talisman.
{178.} To prevent anyone from killing game.
{179.} To compel a thief to return stolen goods.
{180.} A charm against powder and ball.
{181.} Unlucky days.
{182.} Concluding prayer.

APPENDIX.

{183.} A certain cure for epilepsy.
{184.} A salve to heal up wounds.
{185.} Peaches, their medical properties.
{186.} Sweet oil, its virtues.
{187.} Cure for the dropsy.
{188.} Cure for the dropsy, said to be infallible.
{189.} ADDITIONAL. — Cure for the dropsy, effectual.
{190.} Remedy for the lockjaw.
{191.} For the sting of a wasp or bee.
{192.} Diarrhea mixture.
{193.} Soap powders.
{194.} To dye a madder red.
{195.} To dye a fine scarlet red.
{196.} To dye a permanent blue.
{197.} To dye a green.
{198.} Physic ball for horses.
{199.} Physic for cattle.
{200.} Sedative and worm ball.
{201.} Astringent ball for looseness in horses.
{202.} Mixture for ulcers and all foul sores.
{203.} Yellow water in horses.
{204.} A valuable recipe for galls — windgalls in horses.
{205.} Wind-broken horses.

Gypsy Witch Book of Old Pennsylvania Dutch Pow-Wows and Hexes

Gypsy Witch Book of Old Pennsylvania Dutch Pow-Wows and Hexes

Forbidden Secrets of Mystical Knowledge – For Only a Dime
By Tim R. Swartz

IN the late 19th century, there was an explosion of popular books that promised to answer all of your questions about the future and solve all of your personal problems with secret arcane knowledge. These fortune-telling books were filled with page after page of dream interpretations, charms, spells, incantations, and other tidbits of mystic information that had previously been unavailable to the general population.

These books had covers that were guaranteed to draw the eye and inflame the senses with titles such as: *The Old Witch's Dream Book And Complete Fortune Teller*, *Napoleon's Book of Fate and Oraculum*, *Gypsy Witch Fortune Teller by The Queen of Romanies*, *The Ancient and Modern Ladies Oracle*, *Aunt Sally's Policy Players Dream Book*, etc.

They could be found in certain stores, but these kinds of books were also available by mail order and through agents (people who sold products to friends and neighbors). As noted by Catherine Yronwode on the website Luckymojo.com, mystic-themed books were carried by companies such as: King Novelty/Famous Products, Lucky Heart Company of Memphis, and Dorene Publishing Co. of Texas.

Yronwode states that the agents who sold these items for manufacturer-distributors like Valmor-King were usually part-time beauticians and hoodoo root workers.

"They would come to your house to fix your hair (selling you the cosmetics and hair preparations they had bought wholesale) and they would also do psychic consultations and perform rootwork and conjuration, using the curios available from the same sources."

These agents carried their company's retail catalogs with them, and you could order books that were mailed directly to your home.

What is interesting about many of these books is that they were often based on actual grimoires (ancient books of magical spells and information) that were not readily available except to academic scholars. The information contained within these little books were taken from European folk-magic, Mediaeval conjuration, Jewish Kabbalism, Allan Kardecian Spiritism, and even Hindu mysticism. You can find talismans, seals, and sigils taken from European grimoires such as: *The Key of Solomon*, and *The Sixth and Seventh Books of Moses*; Recital of Psalms and selected Biblical verses for magical purposes according to Jewish

Gypsy Witch Book of Old Pennsylvania Dutch Pow-Wows and Hexes

(and later Christian) magical traditions; Prayers, benedictions and "power words" as used in Albertus Magnus's *Egyptian Secrets*.

Naturally the use of magical spells taken from "unchristian" sources such as Jewish Kabbalism was not something that would be widely advertised. In fact, one had to tread very lightly indeed when it came to the whole matter of fortune-telling, magical spells and charms, even if the authors claimed that such incantations came directly from the Bible.

For a long time churches have taught that all magic is inherently evil and that anyone who practices it is to be condemned and possibly even put to death. This has little actually to do with a few verses in the Bible that speak against witches and diviners, and more to do with the churches power base that has held control over the people for centuries.

Magic is generally condemned by most major religions. The King James Version of the Bible has the famous translation "Thou shalt not suffer a witch to live" (Exodus 22:18), and Saul is rebuked by God for seeking advice from a diviner who could contact spirits. In the New Testament and later theology, it is thought that all magic is actually powered by demons, making it even more unacceptable, thus, magic was seen as taboo.

Nevertheless, such taboos, as put forth by the Church, were for the most part ignored when it came to such "parlor games" as fortune-telling and magic spells to attract a lover. It was difficult to conceive how such little paperback books could be anything but simple diversions and pleasant entertainment with friends.

It is amazing to consider the heritage behind these popular little books, information that originally was written centuries before and intended only for a select few, but now available to anyone with just a little money and the desire to learn the forbidden secrets of ancient, mystical knowledge.

KING ZOLTAN'S MYSTIC ORACLE – BASED ON SYSTEMS
OF THE ANCIENTS

Gypsy Witch Book of Old Pennsylvania Dutch Pow-Wows and Hexes

PUBLISHERS NOTE.

King Zoltan was King of all the Romany and lived to the grand age of 120 years and seven months. He never worked a day in his life, nor was he ever bothered by foe, solider, or sheriff. He was beloved by all that stood by him, and he always had plenty of money thru his predictions and wise ways.

A Greeting from King Zoltan to the Dear Reader.

Having lived many years free from worry and despair, it falls upon to reveal the great secrets and hidden knowledge that have been passed down to me by my forbearers. Since this knowledge has afforded me times of absolute joy and happiness, destiny compels that this happiness be shared with those deserving to learn these arcane secrets of the ancients.

Others have taken some of these great teachings and have tried to profit with books claiming to be by their own hand. But do not be taken in by these thieves of the night, their charms and incantations are tainted with the black foulness of greed and deception. The words in this fine book are indeed ancient and true of spirit, given from father to son for untold generations since the times when the angels first brought them from God's loving hand to his chosen people.

I hereby commit to the perusal of the reader a collection of great secrets, sufficient in number as may be deemed needful for any purposes. Knowing, from experience, how many an honest citizen hath been robbed of his entire estate through the machination of bad and malicious people, how many a man hath been tortured and tantalized at night, from early childhood, by wicked people of that ilk; so much so that they could hardly bear it any longer. If you are good and true of heart, the great secrets contained within this little book will release you of all troubles, whether they be troubles of this world, or the worlds of spirits both clean and unclean.

Whenever said remedy is to be applied, in case the house of him whom it is intended to assist is called aloud three times with devotion, and by adding both his Christian and all his other names, the usefulness thereof will be readily enough perceived. Thus it happens that this collection contains a number of curious performances of magic, every one of which is worth far more than the reader pays for this entire book.

For the purpose of rendering a great service to mankind, this book was issued, in order to bridle and check the doings of the spirits of wickedness. Whatever objections may be raised against this book by disbelief and jealousy, these pages will, despite all such objections, contain naught else but truth divine, since Christ himself hath commanded that all ye may perform, ye shall do in the name of God, the Son, and the Holy Spirit, so that the Devil may not possess any power over anything whatso-ever to do his will.

I, therefore, beseech every one, into whose hands this book may come, not to treat the same lightly or to destroy the same, because, by such action, he will defy the will of God. Do not use this book to gain power or take any property that belongs to someone else. Neither will you use this book to bring harm to others in any way. To do so will surely bring about the wraith of God with quick and unmerciful judgment and eternal punishment. So to him who properly esteems and values this book, and never abuses its teachings, will not only be granted the usefulness of its contents, but he will also attain everlasting joy and blessing.

Wherever the "2 N. N." occurs, both the baptismal name and all other names of him whom you intend to help, aid or assist, will have to be added, while the † † † signify the highest name of God, which should always be added in conclusion. Every sympathetic formula should be repeated three times.

So Written By King Zoltan, 22nd of June, 1845

Gypsy Witch Book of Old Pennsylvania Dutch Pow-Wows and Hexes

A WONDERFUL PRAYER TO INSURE A HAPPY AND PROSPEROUS LIFE

Say this prayer every morning upon rising:

This grant God the Father, God the Son, and God the Holy Spirit.

Now I will rise in the name of the Lord, and will wander in his path by his word and will beseech our Savior Christ that he may lend me, upon this very day, three of his angels, for this I pray; the first he may protect me, the other keep me without weapon or arms, the third may keep my body from all harm and keep my soul, my blood and flesh, and keep my courage ever fresh. Whoever is stronger as Jesus Christ, he may approach and assail my flesh and blood. In the name of God the Father, the Son and the Holy Ghost. I praise thee heavenly host.

This may grant God the Father, God the Son, and God the Holy Spirit.

† † †

BENEDICTION TO PROTECT FROM THE DANGERS OF ANY SORT OF WEAPON

Jesus, the true God and man, protect me, N. N., from all sorts of arms and weapons, be they of iron, steel, lead, or be they nails, knives or wood, whatever was made and grew since the birth of Christ, is now forged, or may yet be forged, at any future time, of whatever material. Jesus Christ, the true God and man, protect me, N. N., from murder and from cannon balls, from bullets and swords, from thunder and lightning, fire and water, chains and prison, from poison and sorcery, from mad dogs and from shedding of blood, and from sudden death. Save me, Lord God. Jesus, the true God and man, protect me, N. N., from all sorts of arms and weapons, and all those who desire to overpower me. Cause that all their might and strength to be lost, and be vain.

N. N., hold and aim your armament and sword or lancet toward the cross of Christ and his sacred five wounds, in all my troubles, and at all times; and command all shot and fire-arms that they may fail to give fire; and all swords, spears, lancets, and hellebards, and other pointed instruments, that their edges may become as soft as the blood of Christ, who suffered on the cross. Jesus, protect N. N., wherever I may be, against all enemies, be they visible or invisible, secret or open. The eternal Godhead may save and protect me through the bitter sufferings, death and resurrection of Jesus Christ, and through his holy rose-colored blood, which he shed upon the cross. Jesus begotten at Nazareth, born in Bethlehem, died in Jerusalem, crucified and tortured; these are truthful words, which are written in this letter, that I may not be captured by any murderer, or any other man, be killed, whipped, wounded, nor be laid in fetters; let move away from me, or yield my will. Fly and vanish until I shall recall them, all enemies and all arms, weapons and armament, may they be called by whatever name. None will injure me. Lead and iron projectiles, remain quiet in your armament, for the sake of the martyred Jesus Christ and his holy five wounds. In the name of the Father, the Son and the Holy Spirit. In case a person has a tumor growing, or warts of any kind upon his body, he or she shall go to church and, when he notices two persons speaking to each other, he shall touch the humor or wart, and recite three times: What I see is a great sin and shame, and what I touch may vanish soon.

TO PROTECT ALL POSSESSIONS FROM THIEVES

Speak this every morning three times over all possessions:

Our dear mother in a garden came. Three angels comforted her there. The first is named St. Michael; the other, St. Gabriel; the third, St. Peter. Then spake Peter to our beloved Mary: I saw three thieves enter there. They intend to steal thy dear child and kill it. But the beloved mother Mary said: Peter, bind; St. Peter, bind; and Peter bound them with iron bands, with God's own hands, and with his holy five wounds, for this be with Gabriel, upon this day and night, and this entire year, and forever and all times, my possessions bound. Whoever attempts to steal therefrom, must stand still, like a stick, and see like a brick, and must stand quiet. He must go upward, that he cannot depart from hence until I permit him to proceed from thence. With my own tongue I must tell him this. This is my order and Gabriel's will, which now, by day and night, and all the year, for all times to come, will utter to every thief, for them to repent. For this may God his blessing lend. God the Father, God the Son, and God the Holy Spirit. Amen.

PRAYER TO BE SECURED FROM ALL ASSAILANTS

Now I will Walk over the threshold I met three men, not yet very old. The first was God the Father; the other was God the Son; the third was God the Holy Spirit. They protect my body and soul, blood and flesh, that in no well I fall, that water may not swell me at all, that a rabid dog may never bite me, that shot and stone may never smite me, that spear and knife may never cut me; that never a thief may steal the least from me. Then it shall become like our dear Savior's sweat. Whoever is stronger and mightier than these three men, he may come hither, assail me if he can, or forever keep his peace with me. † † †

TO SECURE AGAINST ATTACK WHILE TRAVELING

Speak three times: *Two wicked eyes have overshadowed me, but three other eyes are overshadowing me too, the one of God, the Father, the other of God the Son, the third of God the Holy Spirit, they watch my blood and flesh, my marrow and bone, and all other large and small limbs, they shall be protected in the name of God the Holy Spirit, God the Father, God the Son.* † † †

TO PREVENT ANYONE FROM DOING EVIL AGAINST YOU

Welcome, in the name of God, ye brethren true and God, we all have drank of the Savior's blood. God the Father be with me; God the Son be with you; God the Holy Spirit be with us all. Let us meet in union and part from each other in peace.

† † † *Three times spoken.*

HOW TO PREDICT THE FUTURE STATE OF THE WEATHER DURING THE YEAR

If New-Year's Day falls upon a Sunday, a quiet and gloomy winter may be expected, followed by a stormy spring, a dry summer, and a rich vintage. When New-Year's Day comes on a Monday, a varied winter, good spring, dry summer, cloudy weather, and an inferior vintage may be expected. When New-Year's comes on a Wednesday, a hard, rough winter, a blustery, dreary spring, an agreeable summer, and a blessed vintage may be hoped for. If the first of the year happens to come on Thursday, a temperate winter, agreeable spring, a dry summer, and a very good vintage will follow. If on a Friday the year begins, a changeable, irregular winter, a fine spring, a dry and comfortable summer, and a rich harvest will be the result. If New-Year's Day comes on Saturday, a rough winter, bleak winds, a wet and dreary spring, and destruction of fruit will be the consequence.

TO OBTAIN MONEY

Take the eggs of a swallow, boil them, return them to the nest, and if the old swallow brings a root to the nest, take it, put it into your purse, and carry it in your pocket, and be happy.

TO OPEN ALL LOCKS

Kill a green frog, expose it to the sun for three days, powder or pulverize it. A little of this powder put into a lock will open the same.

HOW TO DISCERN ALL SECRETS AND INVISIBLE THINGS

If you find a white adder under a hazelnut shrub, which had twelve other vipers as its twelve guardsmen with it, and the hazelnut bush, under which they lay, bears commonly medlers, you must eat the white adder with your other food, and you will be enabled to see and discern all secret and otherwise hidden things.

HOW TO STOP BLEEDING

Jesus born at Bethlehem, Jesus crucified at Jerusalem, as true as these words are, to truly understand N. N. (here call the name of him whom you desire to help) that thy blood will now be stopped, in the name of God the Father, the Son, and the Holy Spirit.

HOW TO CAUSE YOUR INTENDED WIFE TO LOVE YOU

Take feathers from a rooster's tail and press them three times into her hand.

Or: Take a turtle dove tongue into your mouth, talk to your friend agreeably, kiss her and she will love you so dearly that she will never love another.

WHEN YOU WISH THAT YOUR SWEETHEART SHALL NOT DENY YOU

Take the turtle dove tongue into your mouth again and kiss her, and she will accept your suit. **Or:** Take salt, cheese and flour, mix it together, put it into her room, and she will rest not until she sees you.

PRAYER TO HEAL MAN AND BEAST FROM ATTACKS BY EVIL SPIRITS

Thou unclean spirit, thou has attacked N. N.; let that witchcraft recede from him into thy marrow and into thy bone, let it be returned unto thee. I exorcise thee for the sake of the five wounds of Jesus, thou evil spirit, and conjure thee for the five wounds of Jesus of this flesh, marrow and bone; I exorcise thee for the sake of the five wounds of Jesus, at this very hour restore to health again N. N., in the name of God the Father, God the Son, and of God the Holy Spirit. Speak this three times over said victim during three sunrises.

PRAYER TO FOREVER BANISH WICKED PEOPLE

All ye evil spirits, I forbid you my bedstead, my couch; I forbid you, in the name of God, my house and home; I forbid you, in the name of the Holy Trinity, my blood and flesh, my body and soul; I forbid you all the nail holes in my house and home, till you have traveled over every hillock, waded through every water, have counted all the leaflets of the trees, and counted all the starlets in the sky, until that beloved day arrives when the mother of God will bring forth her second Son. † † †

This prayer, three times spoken in the house of the bewitched person, always adding, in the right place, both his baptismal and other names, has been found excellent in many cases.

TO HEAL INJURIES ON MAN, CATTLE OR HORSE

Cut down a burdock bush, and put it into your house, so that it may wither. Then take a thread from a reel which had never been washed, and speak:

Burdock bush, I bind thee that thou shalt heal the injury of this man (or beast, as the case may be), be it boils, sores, gout, swellings, or whatever it may be. Double the thread, and move around the bush, where the thickest part is, in the name of God the Father, and make a knot, then repeat the same in the name of God the Son, and make another knot, and repeat the same motion, while saying in the name of the Holy Spirit, and again make a knot, and say then: What I and thou cannot heal, that may heal the Holy Trinity.

After this, put the bush in a place where no air moves, and the injury will be healed from the root.

TO MAKE ONE'S SELF SHOT PROOF

Dig and stick mouse-ear herb on a Friday, during the half or full of the moon, tie in a white cloth and suspend it from the body. Probatum.

Gypsy Witch Book of Old Pennsylvania Dutch Pow-Wows and Hexes

Or carry these words upon your body:

*LIGHT, BETTER, CLOTENTAL,
SOBATH, ADONAY,
ALBOA, FLOBAT*

TO SEE WHAT OTHERS CANNOT SEE

Take a cat's eye, lay it in salt water, let it remain there for three days, and then for six days into the rays of the sun, after this have it set in silver, and hang it around your neck.

AN AMBROSE-STONE

Steal the eggs of a raven, boil them hard, lay them again into the nest and the raven will fly across the sea and bring a stone from abroad and lay it over the eggs and they will become at once soft again. If such a stone is wrapped up into a bay leaf and is given to a prisoner, that prisoner will be liberated at once. Whoever touches a door with such a stone, to him that door will be opened, and he who puts that stone into his mouth will understand the song of every bird.

WHEN A CHILD IS BEWITCHED

Stand with the child toward the morning sun, and speak:

Be welcome In God's name and sunshine, from whence didst brightly beam, aid me and my dear child and feign my songs serenely stream. To keep the Father sound my praise, help praise the Holy Ghost that he restore my child to health, I praise the heavenly host. † † †

TO ALLAY PAINS WHEREVER THEY BE

Today is a holy sacred day, that God will not cause you any pain to bear, which thou may have on any part of your body, be it man, horse, cattle, or anything living, all the same. I beseech thee. Oh, holy Trinity, help this N. N., that all his pains may cease, whatever they may be called and all that Cometh from evil things. Christ commandeth, Christ vanquisheth, Christ became a being in flesh for thy sake and to protect thee against all evil. Jesus Christ of Nazareth, the crucified Saviour, with Mary his beloved mother, help this N. N. from all evil whatever name it may bear. Amen, † † †   *Jesus Nazarenus Rex Judaeorum.*

TO MAKE A MIRROR IN WHICH EVERYTHING MAY BE DISCERNED

Procure a looking glass, such as are commonly sold. Inscribe the characters noted below upon it. Inter it on the crossing of two pathways, during an uneven hour. On the third day thereafter, return to the place at same hour, and take it out: but you must not be the first person to look into the glass. It is best to let a dog or a cat take the first look into the mirror:

S. Solam S. Tattler S. Echogardner Gematar.

TO ASCERTAIN WHETHER OR NOT A SICK PERSON WILL DIE

Take a piece of bread, place it before the sick one's brow, then throw it before a dog. If he eats it, the patient recovers; if he rejects it, the sick one dies.

TO DRIVE AWAY AND VANQUISH ALL FOES

Whoever carries the hemlock herb, with the heart of a mole, on his person, vanquishes all his enemies, so that they will not be able to trouble him.' Such a man will obtain much. When this herb is laid under the head of a sick person, the sick one, when he sings, will get well; if he cries, he will die.

Gypsy Witch Book of Old Pennsylvania Dutch Pow-Wows and Hexes

WHILE TRAVELING

Say every morning:

Grant me, oh Lord, a good and pleasant hour, that all sick people may recover, and all distressed in body or mind, repose or grace may find, and guardian angel may over them hover; and all those captive and in bondage fettered; may have their conditions and troubles bettered; to all good travelers on horse or foot, we wish a safe journey joyful and good, and good women in labor and toil a safe delivery and joy. † † †

A WAND TO DISCOVER TREASURE

Proceed in the forenoon before twelve o'clock to a hazelnut shrub, which grew within one year and has two twigs, then place yourself toward the rising sun and take the twigs in both hands and speak:

I conjure thee, one summer long, hazel rods by the power of God, by the obedience of Jesus Christ of Nazareth, God and Mary's own son, who died on the cross, and by the power of God, by the truth of God arose from the dead; God the Father, Son and Holy Ghost, who art the very truth thyself, that thou showest me where silver and gold is hidden.

The twigs will now move whenever in the presence of treasure.

HOW TO TELL A PERSON'S FORTUNE WITH CARDS

The Romany have for centuries used this method of telling fortunes with playing cards to make money off of the outsiders. Only those within the tribes know the true secrets of how to use the cards to discern the future. As many of those events about to happen may be easily gathered from the cards, I have here affixed the definition which each card in the pack bears separately; by combining them the reader must judge for himself, observing the following directions in laying them out.

It is worked with a piquet set of ordinary playing cards, which, as most people will know, consists of the usual picture-pieces and the ace, 10, 9, 8 and 7 of each suit, excluding the lower numbers.

DIAMONDS
The Ace. -Letters, or news at hand otherwise.

King. -Friendship; if followed by the Queen, marriage; if reversed, impediments, difficulties and the vexations thereto belonging.

Queen. -A woman from the country, who is fair but evil-speaking; reversed, more directly inimical to the Querent in word and also in deed.

Knave. -A postman, valet, postillion, soldier, or messenger bearing news. The news are good if the card is right side up and bad if it appears reversed. Ten. -Great joy, change of place, a party from the country.

Nine. -Delay and postponement, but not resulting in failure.

Eight. -A man of business or young merchant, who is commercially related to the Querent.

Seven. -Good news, above all if accompanied by the Ace.

HEARTS
The Ace. -Joy, contentment, and if it is accompanied by several picture-cards, marriages, feasts, etc;, in pleasant company.

King. -A rich man, banker, or financier, well disposed, and may promote the interests of the Querent. If reversed, the person is miserly and to deal with him will prove difficult.

Queen. -An honest, frank and obliging woman; if reversed, there will be some obstacle to a projected marriage.

Knave. -A soldier or young man, who is anxious to promote the Querent's welfare, will play some part in his life and will be allied with him after one or another manner.

Ten. -A surprise, but often one of a kind which will be advantageous as well as agreeable to the consulting party.

Nine. -Concord.

Eight. -Domestic and private happiness, attended by success in undertakings; exceedingly felicitous for the destinies of the middle path, the amenities of the quiet life.

Seven. -Marriage, if the Querent is a lady and the issue will be daughters only; if a man, it is destined that he will make a rich and happy marriage.

SPADES

The Ace. -In company with the ten and nine, this card signifies death, grief, more especially from bereavement, but also sorrow from many sources; it includes further the idea of treason and possibly of loss by theft or robbery.

King. -A magistrate or lawyer, whose intervention may prove disagreeable; the card reversed signifies loss in a lawsuit or general derangement of affairs.

Queen. -A disappointed woman – possibly a widow in dejection; if reversed, one who is anxious to remarry, unknown to or in spite of her family.

Knave. -Some kind of disgrace which will be inimical to the peace of mind and perhaps even the liberty of the Querent; reversed, serious complications for the person concerned; also betrayal in love, if the Querent is a woman.

Ten. -Imprisonment for a man, if followed by the Ace and King of the same suit; for a woman, disease, illness.

Nine. -Protraction and difficulties in business; followed by the Nine of Diamonds and the Ace of Clubs, delay in the receipt of expected money.

Eight. -Arrival of a person who will carry bad news if followed by the Seven of Diamonds and near to a picture card- whether King, Queen or Knave- tears, discord, destitution or loss of employment.

Seven. -Quarrels, inquietude; if ameliorated by the vicinity of some Hearts, it promises safety, independence and moral consolation.

CLUBS
The Ace. -Advantages, commercial and industrial benefits of every kind, easy collection of dues, unmixed prosperity – but these more especially when followed by the Seven of Diamonds and the Seven of Clubs.

King. -An influential, powerful person, who is equitable and benevolent towards the Querent, to whom he will render signal services; but reversed this personage will experience some difficulty in his proceedings and may be even in danger of failure.

Queen. -A dark woman, rivalry, competitive spirit; in the neighborhood of a card which stands for a man, she will have preference for the man in question; on the contrary, in proximity to a feminine card, she will be in sympathy with the Querent; reversed, she is very covetous, jealous and disposed to infidelity.

Knave. -One who is in love, a proper young man, who pays court to a young lady; placed next to a feminine card, his chances of success are very good; side by side with a man, there is reason to hope that the latter will come actively to his assistance and will contribute to his success, unless the said man should be signified by the Knave of Hearts, which presages a dangerous rivalry; reversed, there is reason to fear opposition to marriage on the part of the person's parents.

Ten. -Prosperity and good fortune of every kind; at the same time, if followed by the Nine of Diamonds a delay is foreshadowed in the return of money; contrary to all, if this card is side by side with the Nine of Spades – which everywhere signifies disappointment complete failure is promised; so also if the question at stake is a lawsuit, loss is probable.

Nine. -Success in love; for a bachelor or spinster, approaching marriage;

for a widow, her second nuptials.

Eight. -A favorable conclusion which may be anticipated by the Querent in financial and business matters.

Seven. -Anxieties occasioned by love -- intrigues; followed by the Seven of Diamonds and the Nine of Spades, abundance of good things and rich family inheritances.

-SOME EXAMPLES ON HOW THE CARDS CAN BE USED-

FOR MARRIAGE AND AFFAIRS OF THE HEART

Shuffle the cards of a piquet set and cut three times. If an actual marriage is in question, remove two cards, representing the lover and the lady whose fortunes are at issue. Place these cards, face upwards, on the table before you. As usual, fair people are represented by Hearts and Diamonds but those of dark complexion by Clubs and Spades. The attribution, between these lines, seems to be usually at predilection or discretion, but Diamonds are sometimes taken to signify very fair people and blondes, while Spades are for actual brunettes and very dusky complexions.

Lay out the rest of the cards three by three; in every triplicity which produces two of the same suit, select the higher card of that suit and place it by the side of the other card which stands for the Querent. Throw out the rest for the moment, but they will be required later. When any triplicity produces entirely different suits, put aside all three in the rejected pile. When the entire cards of the set have thus been dealt with in succession, take up the rejected lot, and after shuffling and cutting as before, proceed in the same manner until you have drawn fifteen cards and placed them by the side of the Querent.

If the Querent is a dark man, he will not have his wish regarding the marriage contemplated unless a tierce to the King in Clubs be among the fifteen cards. It may of course happen that the King has been drawn to represent him. If, however; he be a Spade, then alternatively there must be a tierce in Spades. The same rule obtains if the Querent is a dark young lady, but in addition to a tierce in the suit there must be the Ace of the suit also.

If the Querent is a fair man or woman, then a tierce in the one case and a tierce and the Ace in the other must be found in Hearts or Diamonds according to the grade of their fairness. If the question concerns a marriage to take place in the country, it has been held by the expositors of the system that a tierce to the King in Diamonds is indispensable. This seems to involve the system in respect of fair people, but it is only a confusion of expression.

If Diamonds correspond to the Querent, that tierce must obviously be present, or there will be no marriage; but if present the inference is that the Querent will get his wish in respect of locality as well as of the fact of marriage. On the other hand, if the Querent is referable to any other of the three remaining suits, then ex hypothesi to attain his presumed wish for a country wedding, he must have the tierce in Diamonds as well as in his own suit.

It is not very probable that the alternative between town and country will arise as a subsidiary question, and if it does, it might be better to determine it separately by the help of some other system. It serves no purpose to ignore the shades of complexion in fair people and represent them indifferently by Diamonds, as this would be forcing the oracles and would make the reading void.

Finally, if the marriage question concerns a widower or widow, it is equally essential that the cards drawn should furnish a tierce to the King in Spades and the Ace of Hearts- which again is very hard upon all persons who are not represented by Spades. The inference is that second marriages are rare.

FOR QUESTIONS ON INHERITANCES

Shuffle and cut as before, and place on the table a card which is held to typify the Querent. The presence of the Ace of Spades, manifesting right side up, indicates profit in consequence of a death that is to say, an inheritance or legacy. If the Ace is accompanied by the Seven, Eight, Nine and Ten of Clubs, there will be a large increment of money. The combination may be difficult to secure, but very large inheritances are rarer than second marriages.

FOR LAWSUITS AND SIMILAR MATTERS

No judgment can be given on the chances of a lawsuit, actual or pending, nor generally on things of this nature, unless the King of Spades comes out in the dealing. If that card is held usually to represent the Querent, then it only follows automatically that a judgment is possible, and it is so much the easier for him in such case. The shuffling, cutting and dealing proceed as before, and if the Ace in question serves to complete the quint major in Spades – that is, the Ace, King, Queen, Knave and Ten – it is to be feared that the suit will prove good for nothing, either by going against the Querent or bringing him no profit in the opposite case. But if the Ace is accompanied by the four Tens, the chances are excellent. They are said also to be more than good in another event of the dealing which I forbear from dwelling on, as it is practically, if not otherwise, impossible for the fifteen cards – which the dealing proposes to extract – to be all of the red suits. It is well known that compilers of works on cartomancy sometimes forget the limits prescribed by their systems and get consequently into ridiculous plights.

FOR A THEFT

For the discovery of a thief, the presence of the four Knaves is indispensable to any reading, and, as it happens, it is not utterly difficult – though it is none too easy – that the chances of the cards should produce them. The procedure is throughout as before. If the King and the Eight of Spades turn up among the fifteen cards, this means that the thief is already in prison; if the Ace of Spades is among them, the prisoner will be in danger of death; the presence of the Ace of Clubs, the King of Clubs and the Queen of Hearts will afford some hope that the person who stole will himself make restitution; lastly, the predominance of Diamonds offers ground for believing that the thief has been arrested, but on another charge than that which would be preferred by the Querent on his own part.

FOR A PERSON IN PRISON

The question at issue is whether the captive has any chance of speedy liberation. The procedure is throughout as before, except that the card selected is held to represent the person in durance instead of the Querent. The fifteen cards having been produced as the result of the working, they should be examined in the usual way. The presence of the Queen of Hearts, Knave of Clubs, Nine of Clubs and the four Aces will give ground for hope that liberation will be easy and at hand.

In proportion as these cards are absent, there will be delay in the desired event, and if none are found, it is likely to be rather remote. On the other hand, the appearance of the Eight and Nine of Spades, the King of Spades, and the Knave and Nine of Diamonds, will signify that liberty shall be scarcely obtained, except after many obstacles and much consequent postponement.

FOR TRAVELERS

It is assumed that the Querent is not himself on a journey but is consulting the oracles for one in whose fortunes he is for some reason interested, by ties of friendship or otherwise. Proceed as before, selecting a card to represent the absent person. When the dealing is finished, the resulting cards should be consulted to ascertain whether they include the Ace of Hearts, the Ace of Diamonds and the Ten of Diamonds, the presence of which will foreshadow probable news. Probability will be raised into certainty by the appearance of the Seven of Diamonds. If, however, the Ten of Spades is found in proximity to the card representing the person who is away on his travels, there will be reason to fear that he is ill; so also the Ace of Spades reversed will mean that he is in other danger than sickness. If he is to succeed in the enterprise that has called him abroad, he will be escorted by the Nine of Hearts, the Ace and the King of Clubs. Finally, if the Eight of Diamonds is found in relation to his own card, this means that he is on the point of returning.

There is a variation of procedure in all the above cases, which consists in protracting the dealing till twenty-one cards have been drawn instead of fifteen. It is suggested that the predominance of red cards as the result of operation in any given instance foretells great success for the person on whose behalf the consultation is made.

The Ace, Ten, Nine, Eight and Seven of Hearts are premonitory of news on which the Querent may be congratulated. The same cards in the suit of Clubs promise success in a lawsuit, or a lucky number in a lottery. The same in the suit of Spades portend news of a relative's death, or that of a friend, but whether there will be profit to the Querent is not so certain, having regard to the generally fatal nature of this suit, the constituents of which may be said almost to constitute the greater misfortunes in cartomancy. The particular numbers in the suit of Diamonds carry with them the same kind of prevision as Hearts.

These are but a few examples of what questions can be answered using the cards. One can create a simple spread of three cards representing the past, present and future that for most, is all that is needed to gain insight on one's future.

Another way is to only reverse the aces, as these are called the points, and are of most particular consequence; then take out the eights, for they are cards of no meaning; you will then nave twenty-eight left, which you must thus manage: shuffle them well, and deal them into four equal parcels; having first decided of what suit you will be the queen, and you must make your lover, or husband, of the same suit as yourself without regard to his complexion; take up the parcel dealt exactly before you, and then proceed regularly round to the right, examining them separately as you proceed. The first tells what is to happen soon, the second at some distance, and the third respects your husband or lover, and the fourth your secret wishes.

Gypsy Witch Book of Old Pennsylvania Dutch Pow-Wows and Hexes

CHARMS, SPELLS AND INCANTATIONS THAT ARE TO BE RESORTED TO AT CERTAIN SEASONS OF THE YEAR, TO PROCURE BY DREAMS AN INSIGHT INTO FUTURITY, PARTICULARLY IN REGARD TO THE ARTICLE OF MARRIAGE

ST. AGNES DAY

Falls on the 21st of January; you must prepare yourself by a twenty-four hours' fast, touching nothing but pure spring water, beginning at midnight on the 20th to the same again on the 21st; then go to bed, and mind you sleep by yourself; and do not mention what you are trying to any one, or It will break the spell; go to rest on your leftside, and repeat these lines three times:

St. Agnes be a friend to me
In the gift I ask of thee;
Let me this night my husband see -

and you will dream of your future spouse. If you see more men than one in your dream, you will wed two or three times, but, if you sleep and dream not, you will never marry.

ST. MAGDALEN

Let three young women assemble together on the eve of this saint in an upper apartment, where they are sure not to be disturbed, and let no one try whose age is more than twenty-one, or it breaks the charm; get rum, wine, gin, vinegar, and water, and let each have a hand in preparing the potion. Put it in a ground-glass vessel; no other will do. Then let each young woman dip a sprig of rosemary in, and fasten It in her bosom, and, taking three sips of the mixture, get into bed; and the three must sleep together, but not a word must be spoken after the ceremony begins, and, you will have time dreams, and of such a nature that you cannot possibly mistake your future destiny. It is not particular us to the hour in which you retire to rest.

THE CHARMS OF ST. CATHERINE

This day falls on the 25th of November, and must be thus celebrated. Let any number of young women, not exceeding seven or less than three, assemble in a room, where they are sure to be safe from interlopers; just as the clock strikes eleven at night, take from your bosom a sprig of myrtle, which you must have worn there all day, and fold it up in a bit of tissue paper, then light up a small chafing dish of charcoal, and on it let each maiden throw nine hairs from her head, and a paring of her toe and finger nails, then let each sprinkle a small quantity of myrtle and frankincense in the charcoal, and while the odoriferous vapor rises, fumigate your myrtle (this plant, or tree is consecrated to Venus) with it go to bed while the clock is striking twelve, and you will be sure to dream of your future husband, and place the myrtle exactly under your head. Observe, it is no manner of use trying this charm, if you are not a real virgin, and the myrtle hour of performance must be passed in strict silence.

HOW TO MAKE YOUR LOVER OR SWEETHEART COME TO YOU

If a maid wishes to see her lover, let her take the following method. Prick the third, or wedding finger of your left hand with a sharp needle (beware a pin), and with the blood write your own and lover's name on a piece of clean writing paper in as small a compass as you can, and encircle it with three round rings of the same crimson stream, fold it up, and at exactly the ninth hour of the evening, bury it with your hand bury it within the earth, and tell no one. Your lover will hasten to you as soon as possible, and he will not be able to rest until he sees you, and if you have quarreled, to make it up. A young man may also try this charm, only instead of the wedding finger; let him pierce his left thumb,

APPLE PARINGS

On the 28th of October, which is a double Saint's day, take an apple, pare it whole, and take the paring in your right hand, and standing in the middle of the room say the following verse:

St. Simon and Jude,
On you I intrude,
By this paring I hold to discover,
Without any delay,
To tell me this day,
The first letter of my own true lover.

Turn round three times, and cast the paring over your left shoulder, and it will form the first letter of your future husband's surname; but if the paring breaks into many pieces, so that no letter is discernible, you will never marry; take the pips of the same apple, put them in spring water, and drink them.

TO KNOW HOW SOON A PERSON WILL BE MARRIED

Get a green pea-pod, in which are exactly nine peas, hang it over the door, and then take notice of the next person who comes in, who is not of the family, and if it proves a bachelor, you will certainly be married within that year.

On any Friday throughout the year – take rosemary flowers, bay leaves, thyme, and sweet marjoram, of each a handful; dry these and make them into a fine powder; then take a tea-spoon-fill of each sort, mix the powders together; then take twice the quantity of barley flour and make the whole into cake with the milk of a red cow.
This cake is not to be baked, but wrapped in clean writing paper, and laid under your head any Friday night. If the person dreams of music, she will wed those she desires, and that shortly; if of fire, she will be crossed in love; if of a church, she will die single. If any thing is written or the least spot of ink is on the paper, it will not do.

TO KNOW WHAT FORTUNE YOUR FUTURE HUSBAND WILL BE

Take a walnut, a hazel-nut, and nutmeg; grate them together, and mix them with butter and sugar, and make them up into small pills, of which exactly nine must be taken on going to bed; and according to her dreams, so will be the state of the person she will marry. If a gentleman, of riches; if a clergyman, of white linen; if a lawyer, of darkness; if a tradesman, of odd noises and tumults; if a soldier or sailor, of thunder and lightning; if a servant, of rain.

A CHARM FOR DREAMING

When you go to bed, place under your pillow a Common Prayer Book, open at the part of the Matrimonial service, in which is printed, "With this ring I thee wed," etc., place on a key, a ring, a flower and a sprig of willow, a small heart cake, a crust of bread, and the following cards, the ten of clubs, nine of hearts, ace of spades, and the ace of diamonds; wrap all these round in a handkerchief of thin gauze or muslin, on getting into bed cram your hoods and say:

Luna ever woman's friend,
To me thy goodness condescend;
Let me this night in visions see,
Emblems of my destiny.

If you dream of storms, trouble will betide you; if the atom ends in a fine calm, so will your fate; if of a ring, or of the act of diamonds, marriage; bread, an industrious life; cake, a pros perous life; flowers, joy; willow, treachery in love; spades, death; diamonds, money; clubs, a foreign land; hearts, illegitimate children; keys, that you will rise to great trust and power, and never know want; birds, that you will have many children, geese, that you will marry more than once.

THE FLOWER AUGURY

If a young man or woman receives a present of flowers, or a nosegay from, their sweetheart, unsolicited, for if asked for, it destroys the influence of the spell; let them keep them in the usual manner in cold water four-and-twenty hours, then shift the water, and let them stand another twenty-four hours, then take them, and immerse the stalks in water nearly boiling, leave them to perish for three hours. If they are perished, or drooping, your lover is false; if revived and blooming, you will be happy in your choice.

HOW TO TELL BY A SCREW, WHETHER YOUR SWEETHEART LOVES YOU OR NOT

Get a small screw, such as the carpenters use for hanging closet-doors, and after making a hole in a plank with a gimlet of a proper size, put the screw in, being careful to oil the end with a little sweet oil. After having done this, take a screw-driver and drive the screw home, but you must be sure and observe how many turns it takes to get the screw in so far that it will go no farther. If it requires an odd number of turns you can rest assured that your sweetheart does not love you yet, and perhaps is enamored of some other person; but if the number of turns is an even number, be happy, for your sweetheart adores you, and lives only in the sunshine of your presence.

STRANGE BED

Lay under your pillow a prayer-book, opened at the Matrimonial Service, bound round with the garters you wore that day and a sprig of myrtle, on the page that says, "with this ring I thee wed," and your dream will be ominous, and you will have your fortune as well told as if you had paid a crown to an astrologer.

A SPELL - (To be used at any convenient time)

Make a nosegay of various colored flowers, one of a sort, a sprig of rue. and some yarrow off a grave, and bind all together with the hair from your head; sprinkle them with a few drops of the oil of amber, using your left hand, and bind the flowers round your head under your night-cap when you retire to rest; put on clean sheets and linen, and your future mate will appear in your dream.

Gypsy Witch Book of Old Pennsylvania Dutch Pow-Wows and Hexes

PROMISE OF MARRIAGE

If you receive a written one, or any declaration to that effect in a letter, prick the words with a sharp-pointed needle on a sheet of paper quite clear from any writing; fold in nine folds, and place it under your head when you retire to rest. If you dream of diamonds, castles, or even a clear sky, there is no deceit and you will prosper. Trees in blossom, or flowers, show children; washing, or graves, show you will lose them by death; and water shows they are faithful, but that you will go through severe poverty with the party for some time, though all may end well.

TO KNOW YOUR HUSBAND'S TRADE

Exactly at twelve, on Midsummer-day, place a bowl of water in the sun, pour in some boiling pewter as the clock is striking, saying:

Here I try a potent spell, Queen of love and Juno tell, In kind love to me, What my husband Is to be; This the day, and this the hour. When it seems you have the power or to be a maiden's friend. So, good ladies, condescend.

A tobacco-pipe full is enough. When the pewter is cold, take it out of the water, and drain it dry in a cloth, and you will find the emblems of your future husband's trade quite plain. If more than one, you will marry-twice; if confused and no emblems, you will never marry; a coach shows a gentleman for you.

A CHRISTMAS SPELL

Steep mistletoe berries, to the number of nine, in a mixture of ale, wine, vinegar, and honey; take them on going to bed, and you will dream of your future lot; a storm in this dream is very bad; it is most likely that you will marry a sailor, who will suffer shipwreck at sea; but to see either sun, moon, or stars is an excellent presage; so are flowers; but a coffin is an unfortunate index of a disappointment in love.

THE NINE KEYS

Get nine small keys; they must all be your own by begging or purchase (borrowing will not do, nor must you tell what you want them for); plait a three-plaited braid of your own hair, and tie them together, fastening the ends with nine knots; fasten them with one of your garters to your left wrist on going to bed, and bind the other garter round your head; then say:

St. Peter take it not amiss, To try your favor I've done this; You are the ruler of the keys, Favor me, then, if you please; Let me then your influence prove, And see my dear and wedded love.

This must be done on the eve of St. Peter's. It is an old charm used by the maidens of Rome In ancient times, who put great faith in it.

THE THREE KEYS

Purchase three small keys, each at a different place, and, on going to bed, tie them together with your garter, and place them in your left hand glove, along with a small flat dough cake, on which you have pricked the first letters of your sweetheart's name; put them on your bosom when you retire to rest; if you are to have that young man, you will dream of him, but not else.

TO KNOW IF A WOMAN WITH CHILD WILL HAVE A GIRL OR A BOY

Write the proper names of the father and the mother, and the mouth she conceived with child; count the letters in these words, and divide the amount by seven; and then, if the remainder be even, it will be a girl; if uneven, it will be a boy.

Gypsy Witch Book of Old Pennsylvania Dutch Pow-Wows and Hexes

TO KNOW IF A CHILD NEW-BORN SHALL LIVE OR NOT

Write the proper names of the father and mother, and of the day the child was born; count the letters in these words, and to the amount add twenty-five, and then divide the whole by seven; if the remainder be even, the child shall die, but if it be uneven, the child shall live.

A CHARM
(To be used on the eve of any fast directed in the calendar)

This takes a week's preparation, for you must abstain from meat or strong drink. Go not to bed till the clock has struck the midnight hour, and rise before seven the next morning, the whole seven days. You must neither play at cards, or any game of chance, nor enter a place of public diversion. When you go to bed on the night of trial, eat something very salty, and do not drink after it, and you may depend on having very singular dreams; and, being very thirsty, you will probably dream of liquids. Wine is excellent, and shows wealth or promotion; brandy, foreign lands; rum, that you will wed a sailor, or one that gets his living at sea; gin, but a middling life; cordials, variety of fortune; and water, if you drink it, poverty; but to see a clear stream is good. Children are not good to behold in this dream, nor cards, nor dice; they forebode the loss of reputation, or that you will never marry.

VALENTINE

If you receive one of those love tokens, and cannot guess at the party who sent it, the following method will explain it to a certainty. Prick the fourth finger on your left hand, and, with a crow quill, write on the back of the valentine the year, day and hour on which you were born, also the present year. Try this on the first Friday after you receive the valentine, but do not go to bed till midnight; place the paper in your left shoe, and put it under your pillow; lay on your left side, and repeat three times:

St. Valentine, pray condescend To be this night a maiden's friend; Let me now my lover see. Be he of high or low degree; By a sign his station show, Be it weal or be it woe; Let him come to my bedside, And my fortune thus decide.

The young woman will be sure to dream of the identical person who sent the valentine, and may guess, by the other particulars of the dream, if or not he is to be her spouse.

YARROW

This is a weed commonly found in abundance on graves towards the close of the spring and beginning of the summer. It must be plucked exactly on the first hour of morn; place three sprigs either in your shoe or glove, saying:

Good morning, good morning, good yarrow, And thrice a good morning to thee; Tell me before this time tomorrow Who my true love is to be.

Observe, a young man must pluck the weed off a young maiden's grave, and a female must select that of a bachelor's; retire home to bed without speaking a word, or it dissolves the spell; put the yarrow under your pillow, and it will procure a sure dream, on which you may depend.

TO KNOW WHETHER A WOMAN SHALL HAVE THE MAN SHE WISHES

Get two lemon peels and wear them all day, one in each pocket, and at night rub the four posts of the bedstead with them; if she Is to succeed, the person will appear in her sleep, and present her with a couple of lemons; if not, there Is no hope.

TO KNOW IF ANYONE SHALL ENJOY THEIR LOVE OR NOT

Take the number of the first letter of your name, the number of the planet, and the day of the week; put all these together, and divide them by thirty; if it be above, it will come to your mind, and if below, to the contrary; and mind that number which exceeds not thirty.

SIGNS TO CHOOSE GOOD HUSBANDS AND WIVES

1. If the party be of a ruddy complexion, high and full-nosed, his eyebrows bending arch-wise, his eyes standing full, of a black and lively color, it denotes him good-natured, ingenious, and born to good fortune, and the like in a woman, if born under the planet Jupiter.

2. If the party be phlegmatic, lean, and of a dusky complexion, given much to musing and melancholy, beware of such a one, of what sex soever.

3. An indifferent wide mouth, and full cheeks, smooth forehead, little ears, dark-brown hair, and a chin proportionate to the face, is very promising.

4. An extraordinarily long chin, with the underlip larger than the upper, signifies a cross-grained person, fit for little business, yet given to folly.

5. A well-set, broad chin in a man, his face being round, and not too great, and a dimple or dent in a woman's cheek or chin denotes they will come together and live happily.

PREDICTIONS CONCERNING CHILDREN BORN ON ANY DAY OF THE YEAR

SUNDAY-The child born on Sunday will obtain great riches, be long-lived, and enjoy much happiness.

MONDAY-Children born on this day will not be very successful in most enterprises they may engage in, being irresolute, subject to be imposed upon through their good-natured disposition; they are generally willing and ready to oblige every one who asks a favor from them.

Gypsy Witch Book of Old Pennsylvania Dutch Pow-Wows and Hexes

TUESDAY-The person born on this day will be subject to violent starts of passion, and not easily reconciled; if a man, given to illicit connections, from which conduct many serious consequences and misfortunes will arise, and lie will never be safe, being in danger of suffering death by violence, if lie does not put a restraint upon his vicious inclinations.

WEDNESDAY-The child ushered into the world on this day will be of a studious and sedate turn of mind; and if circumstances will allow, fond of perusing the literary works of the most talented ancient and modern authors. Should facilities be afforded to such a one, there is every probability of his being a highly-gifted author.

THURSDAY-Those who first see the light on this day may in general have applied to them the appellation of being "born with a silver spoon in their mouths"; for unless they resolutely spurn from them the Plutonic deity, riches will be poured into their lap with no discerning hand.

FRIDAY-The little stranger who first inhales the vital air on this day will be blessed with a strong constitution, and will be lucky in every enterprise through life, happy in his or her domestic relations, and finally die rich and lamented.

SATURDAY-This is an unlucky day for being ushered into this world of sin and sorrow; but those born on this last day of the week may become good members of society, honored and respected by their fellow-creatures, and blessed by the Almighty.

TO DISCOVER A THIEF BY THE SIEVE AND SHEAR

Stick the points of the shears In the wood of the sieve, and let two persons support it, balanced upright, with their two fingers; then read a certain chapter in the Bible, and afterwards ask St. Peter and St. Paul if A or B is the thief, naming all the persons you suspect. On naming the real thief, the sieve will suddenly turn round about.

Gypsy Witch Book of Old Pennsylvania Dutch Pow-Wows and Hexes

SIGN OF A SPEEDY MARRIAGE AND SUCCESS ATTENDING IT BY SUNDAY SIGNS

1. For a woman to have the first and last letters of her Christian name the same with the man's surname that makes love to her denotes a great union and a generous love.

2. For a man to have the first and last letters of his Christian name the same with the woman's surname denotes the some.

3. To think on a party on a sudden awaking, without any meditation, on a Friday morning that before had a place in the affection of man or woman is a demonstration of love or extraordinary friendship.

4. If a ring falls accidentally off a man's finger that is under no obligation of marriage and runs directly to the feet of a maid or widow, it denotes that he is not only in love with the widow, but that a sudden marriage will ensue.

5. The singing of a robin red-breast at your window, in the time of courtship, on a Wednesday, is a sign that you shall have the party desired.

6. If when walking abroad with your sweetheart, you perceive a pair of pigeons circle you round, it is a sign of marriage and happiness to ensue, with much content.

7. If a hare cross you on a Saturday morning, it promises happy days, riches, and pleasure.

ANCIENT METHODS TO KNOW THE WEATHER

In the evening when the horizon in the West is tinged with a ruddy glow, it is a sign that bright and dry weather will speedily follow.

When the sky appears ruddy in the East in the evening, changeable weather may be confidently anticipated.

Gypsy Witch Book of Old Pennsylvania Dutch Pow-Wows and Hexes

Should the horizon in the North wear a ruddy appearance in the evening, stormy and boisterous weather may be expected.

When the rays from the sun at mid-day are more than ordinarily dazzling, rainy weather will shortly succeed.

In summer-time, when the swallows fly near to the ground, rainy weather will assuredly soon follow.

The shrill crowing of the cock during rainy weather is a sign that drought will speedily prevail.

When the smoke from the chimney falls down towards the ground, instead of rising upwards, it is a sign that rainy weather will soon follow.

When the face of the moon is partially obscured by a light thin vapor, rain will shortly follow.

If on a foggy morning in summer the fog rises upwards, it will be a fine day; if the fog falls to the ground, it will be wet.

When you see the fowls in a farm-yard flocking together under some covert, be assured that ungenial weather is about to succeed.

When the rooks, on flying over your head, make an extraordinary and discordant cawing, rain will come on shortly.

When you see your dog or cat more than ordinarily restless, frisking about the house in all directions, be assured that some boisterous weather will shortly succeed.

In rainy weather, when you hear the chirping of the sparrows on the house-top more shrill than usual, it is a sign that clear and dry weather will quickly succeed.

When you see a vapory fluid resting upon a stagnant pond on the fore-part of the day, you may conclude that rainy weather will shortly come on. Should the vapor ascend and clear away, a continued drought may be anticipated.

In summer, when the atmosphere is dense and heavy, and there is scarcely a breath of air, be assured that a thunder-storm is coming on.

When the firmament is lighted up with meteoric phenomena, such as failing stars, globes of fire, etc., changeable and boisterous weather may be expected to prevail.

When the rising sun appears like a solid mass of fervent-heated metal, and no rays appear to emanate there from, fine and dry weather may be confidently anticipated.

When the sun sets in a halo of ruddy brightness, genial and bright weather may be fully relied on for the coming day.

When the moon appears of a ruddy hue, stormy and boisterous weather may be expected to follow.

When the stars appear of a sparkling brightness, fine and genial weather may be expected to prevail for some time. Should the stars appear obscure and dim, changeable and rainy weather may be anticipated.

When, in summer-time, yon see the cattle grazing in a field gathering together in groups, be assured that a thunder-storm is approaching.

The luminous appearance of the Aurora Borealis, or Northern Lights, foretells the approach of stormy and boisterous weather.

When the Betting sun in the autumn or winter seasons appears ruddy, it is a sign that high and boisterous winds may be expected to blow from, the North and Northwest. When the sun at its rising in the autumn or winter seasons appears ruddy, it foretells that high and boisterous winds may be anticipated to blow from the South and Southeast

When the sea-birds are observed flocking towards the shore, storms and tempests may be confidently expected.

When, in the early autumn season, the migratory birds are seen flocking together, and raking their departure, it is a certain sign that rough and boisterous weather is approaching, and that a severe winter may be anticipated.

When the doves around a dove-cote make a more than ordinary cooing, and frequently pass in and out of their cote, it is a sign that a change of weather is near.

When the robin approaches your habitation, it is a sign that wintry weather will shortly prevail.

When there is a thick vapory mist resting on the tops of high hills in the morning, and remains there during the day, it is a sign that wet and ungenial weather may be anticipated, should the mist eventually rise upward, and be evaporated by the sun's rays, a return to fine, dry weather may be looked for; if, how-aver, the mist falls down into the valley, a continuation of wet weather will prevail.

SIGNS AND OMENS: AUGURIES AND FOREWARNINGS

However skeptical some persons may pro fess to be on the subject of signs, auguries, and forewarnings, still few will venture to deny that in innumerable instances those mysterious admonitions and forewarnings have been speedily followed by events of a pleasant or a painful nature to those who have received them. The belief in signs and auguries has been cherished by mankind ever since the creation; and this faculty is not confined to the human family alone, but the lower animals possess some of them in an extraordinary degree. The following are a few of the multifarious signs and auguries which admonish and forewarn mankind, at one time or another:

Should you suddenly be the subject of a deep depression of spirits, contrary to your usual constitutional buoyancy and liveliness, it is a sure

Gypsy Witch Book of Old Pennsylvania Dutch Pow-Wows and Hexes

sign that you are about to receive some agreeable news or other happy correspondence.

If the crown of your head itches more than ordinary, you may expect to be advanced to a more honorable position in life. Should the hair on your head come off, when combing, in greater quantities than usual, it is a sign that you will soon be the subject of a severe attack of affliction.

If your right eyebrow should immoderately itch, be assured that you are going to look upon a pleasant sight – a long-absent friend, or a long-estranged, but now reconciled, lover.

Should your left eye-brow be visited with a tantalizing itching, it is a sign that you will soon look upon a painful sight – the corpse of a valued friend, or your lover walking with a favored rival.

A ringing in your right ear is an augury that you will shortly hear some pleasant news.

A ringing in your left ear is a sign that you will in a short time receive intelligence of a very unpleasant nature. When your left ear tingles some one is back-biting you.

A violent itching of the nose foretells trouble and sorrow to those who experience it.

An itching of the lips in a sign that some one is speaking disrespectfully of you.

When you are affected by an itching on the back of your neck, be assured that either yourself or some one nearly related to you is about to suffer a violent death.

An itching on the right shoulder signifies that you will shortly have a large legacy bequeathed to you.

When you feel an itching sensation on your left shoulder, be sure that you are about to bear a heavy burden of sorrow and trouble.

Gypsy Witch Book of Old Pennsylvania Dutch Pow-Wows and Hexes

If your right elbow joint itches, you may expect shortly to hear some intelligence that will give you extreme pleasure.

Should you be annoyed with a violent itching on your left elbow joint, you may be sure that some vexatious disappointment will be experienced by you,

If you feel an itching on the palm of your right hand, you may expect soon to receive some money which you have been long expecting.

When the palm of your left hand itches, you may expect to be called upon to pay some money for a debt which you have not personally incurred.

An itching on the spine of your back is a sign that you will shortly be called upon to bear a heavy burden of sorrow and trouble.

An itching on your loins is an indication that you will soon receive an addition to your family, if married; if single, that you are on the eve of marriage.

When you are affected with an itching on the belly; expect to be invited to feast upon a choice collection of savory meats.

When either or both of your thighs itch, be assured that you are about to change your sleeping apartment.

If you have an itching sensation in your right knee, depend upon it that you will shortly undergo a remarkable and beneficial change in your previous course of life, and become religiously inclined.

If a similar sensation prevails in your right knee, you may expect to undergo a change in your deportment of an unfavorable nature.

An itching sensation on the shins foretells that you will be visited with a painful and long-continued affliction.

When your ankle-joints itch, be sure that you are about to be united to one whom you love, if single; if married, that your domestic comforts will be largely increased.

When the sole of your right foot itches, you may feel assured that you are about to undertake a journey from which you will derive much pleasure and enjoyment.

Should you experience a similar sensation on the sole of your left foot, you may expect to be called upon to take a journey of an unpleasant and melancholy nature.

If, in taking a walk, you should see a single magpie, it is a bad omen, especially if it should fly past you to the left hand; but if it should pass you to the right hand, the good will counterbalance the bad. Should you see two magpies together, expect to hear of something to your advantage – a proposal of marriage, if single; or a legacy of money bequeathed to you. Should the magpies fly past you together to your right hand, your own marriage, or the marriage of some one nearly related to you, will occur in a short time. The seeing of several magpies together is considered a very fortunate omen.

May is considered an unlucky month to marry in; therefore avoid doing so if possible. If you can catch a snail by the horns on the first of May, and throw it over your shoulders, you will be lucky throughout the year. If you place one on a slate on that day, it will describe by its turnings the initials of your future partner's name.

If a young man or young woman, on going up a flight of stairs, should stumble in the middle of the flight, it is a sign that his or her marriage will take place in a short time. If the stumbling should be near the top of the stairs, then his or her marriage will be immediately consummated.

If a young person, when seated at the tea-table, should observe one or more stalks of the tea-plant in the newly-poured-out cup, and if, on stirring the tea and holding the spoon in the middle of the liquid, the stalk or stalks should come close to the spoon handle, it is a token that he or she will be soon married.

Gypsy Witch Book of Old Pennsylvania Dutch Pow-Wows and Hexes

When the house-dog is unusually restless, and howls dismally in the night-time, it is a sign that sickness and death are about to visit the family to whom the dog belongs.

When the wick of your candle shows a bright spark in the midst of the flame, it is a sign that a long-absent friend is about to visit you.

When the ribs of your fire-grate are more than usually covered with flukes of soot, it is a sign that a stranger is about to visit your habitation.

If a person stumbles when leaving his house at the beginning of a journey, or trips or stumbles more than once during the course of the journey, it is advisable to postpone it.

It is bad luck to sweep the kitchen floor after dark, and you are sweeping out good luck if you sweep dirt out the door.

If you burn beef bones by mistake it is a sign of much sorrow to come on account of poverty. To burn fish or poultry bones indicates that scandal will be spread about you.

To cross two forks accidentally is a sign that slander will be spread about you. To stir anything with a fork is to stir up misfortune. As well, crossing two table-knives by accident portends bad luck.

To be completely naked in your dream is a very lucky omen. If only your feet are bare, you will have many difficulties to overcome before you can reach your goal. Also, to dream of someone smoking a cigar indicates that money is on its way.

If you involuntarily make a rhyme, that is a lucky omen. Before speaking again, make a wish, and the chances are that it will come true.

It is a sign of good luck if you first see the new moon over your left shoulder, but of bad luck if you see it over your right. Should you have money in your pocket at the time of the new moon, you will be penniless before the moon is in the full.

Gypsy Witch Book of Old Pennsylvania Dutch Pow-Wows and Hexes

To sneeze three times in rapid succession is considered by some to be a good omen.

It is a sure sign that your plans will meet with success if three bees alight on you at the same time.

If you find a coin, you should spit on it to bring good luck.
If the palm of the left hand itches you will be getting money; if the right palm itches, you will be losing/spending money.

A dog passing between a couple about to be married means ill fortune will befall the couple. However, being followed by a strange dog indicates good luck.

FORTUNE TELLING BY THE GROUNDS IN A TEA OR COFFEE CUP

Pour the grounds of tea or coffee into a white cup; shake them well about, so as to spread them over the surface; reverse the cop to drain away the superfluous contents, and then exercise jour fertile fancy in discovering what the figures thus formed represent Long, wavy lines denote vexatious and losses-their importance depending on the number of lines. Straight ones, on the contrary, foretell peace, tranquility, and long life.

Human figures are usually good omens, announcing love affairs, and marriage.

If circular figures predominate, the person for whom the experiment is made may expect to receive money. If these circles are connected by straight, unbroken lines, there will be delay, but ultimately all will be satisfactory, Squares, foretell peace and happiness; oblong figures, family discord; whilst curved, twisted, or angular ones, are certain signs of vexations and annoyances, their probable duration being determined by the number of figures.

A crown signifies honor; a cross, news of death; a ring, marriage—if a letter can be discovered near it that will be the initial of the name of the future spouse. If the ring is in the clear part of the cup, it foretells happy union; if clouds are about it, the contrary; but if it should chance to be quite at the bottom, then the marriage will never take place.

A leaf of clover, or trefoil, is a good sign, denoting, if at the top of the cup, speedy good fortune, which will be more or less distant in case it appears at, or Dear the bottom.

The anchor, if at the bottom of the cup, denotes success in business; at the top, and in the clear part, love and fidelity; but in thick, or cloudy parts, inconstancy.

The serpent is always the sign of an enemy, and if in the cloudy part, gives warning that great prudence will be necessary to ward off misfortune.

The coffin portends news of a death, or long illness.

The dog, at the top of the cup, denotes true and faithful friends; in the middle, that they are not to be trusted; but at the bottom, that they are secret enemies.

The lily, at the top of the cup, foretells a happy marriage; at the bottom, anger.

A letter signifies news; if in the dear, very welcome ones; surrounded by dots, a remittance of money; but if hemmed in by clouds, bad tidings, and losses. A heart near it denotes a love letter. A single portends restoration to health; a group of trees in the dear; misfortunes, which may be avoided; several trees, wide apart, promise that your wishes 'will be accomplished; if encompassed by dashes, it is a token that your fortune is in its blossom, and only requires care to bring to maturity; if surrounded by dots, riches.

Mountains signify either friends or enemies, according to their situation.

The sun, moon, and stars, denote happiness, success. The clouds, happiness or misfortune, according as they are bright or dark.

Birds are good omens, but quadrupeds-with the exception of the dog- foretell trouble and difficulties.

Fish; imply good news from across the water.

A triangle portends an unexpected legacy; a single straight line, a journey.

The figure of a man, indicates a speedy visitor; if the arm is outstretched, a present; when the figure is very distinct, it shows that the person expected will be of dark complexion, and vice versa.

A crown, near a cross, indicates a large fortune, resulting from a death. Flowers are signs of joy, happiness, and peaceful life.

A heart, surrounded by dots, signifies joy, occasioned by the receipt of money; with a ring near it, approaching marriage.

HOW TO READ YOUR FORTUNE BY THE WHITE OF AN EGG

Break a new-laid egg, and, carefully separating the yolk from the white, drop the latter into a large tumbler half full of water; place this, uncovered, in some dry place, and let it remain untouched for four-and-twenty hours, by which time the white of the egg will have formed itself into various figures-rounds, squares, ovals, animals, trees, crosses, which are to be interpreted in the same manner as those formed by the coffee grounds. Of course, the more whites there are in the glass, the more figures there will be.

This is a very interesting experiment, and much practiced by the young Scotch maidens, who, however, believe it to have more efficacies when tried on either Midsummer Eve or Halloween.

USING AN EGG TO REMOVE BAD LUCK

If you are plagued by evil spells and bad luck, try this powerful, ancient spell to help you remove any bewitchment from your life. You must purchase a brown fresh egg before noon of that day. Make sure that you start this when the moon is waning. It is very important that this egg be fresh. Place this egg in a brown bag and tie the neck of the bag with a black cloth string. Place this bag under your bed.

Each night before retiring to bed, you must open this bag and take the egg out and rub it all over your body. When done, put the egg back into the bag, take a deep breath and blow three times into the bag. When you are blowing into the bag, you must imagine that all the bad luck is leaving your body through your breath.

When done, place the bag back under your bed. Do this for nine days. At the end of nine days, take the bag with the egg and dispose of it outside your home.

Each time that you blow into the bag, you must immediately tie it back up. If by the end of seven days you notice that your bag is moving on its own. Stop, and dispose of the bag immediately. Do not look into the bag and make sure that the bag is secure. Only do this if you are serious about removing bad luck and evil bewitchments in your life.

HOW TO TELL FORTUNES BY THE MOLES ON A PERSON'S BODY

1. A mole that stands on the right side of the forehead, or tight temple, signifies that the person will arrive to sudden wealth and honor.

2. A mole on the right eyebrow, announces speedy marriage, the husband to possess many good qualities and a large fortune.

3. A mole on the left of either of those three places, portends unexpected disappointment in your most sanguine wishes.

4. A mole on the outside of either eye, denotes the person to be of a steady, sober, and sedate disposition.

5. A mole on either cheek, signifies that the person never shall rise

Gypsy Witch Book of Old Pennsylvania Dutch Pow-Wows and Hexes

above mediocrity in point of fortune.

6. A mole on the nose, shows that the person will have good success in his or her undertakings.

7. A mole on the lip, either upper or lower, proves the person to be fond of delicate things, and much given to the pleasures of love, in which he or she will most commonly be successful.

8. A mole on the chin, indicates that the person will be attended with great prosperity, and be highly esteemed.

9. A mole on the side of the neck, shows that the person will narrowly escape suffocation; but will afterward rise to great consideration by an unexpected legacy or inheritance.

10. A mole on the throat, denotes that the person shall become rich, by marriage.

11. A mole on the right breast, declares the person to be exposed to a sudden reverse from comfort to distress, by unavoidable accidents. Most of his children will be girls.

12. A mole on the left breast, signifies success in undertakings and an amorous disposition. Most of his children will be boys.

13. A mole on the bosom, portends mediocrity of health and fortune.

14. A mole under the left breast, over the heart, foreshows that a man will be of a warm disposition, unsettled in mind, fond of rambling, and light in his conduct. In a lady it shows sincerity in love, and easy travail in child-birth.

15. A mole on the right side over any part of the ribs, denotes the person to be pusillanimous, and slow in understanding any thing that may be attended with difficulties.

16. A mole on the belly, shows the person to be addicted to sloth and

gluttony, and not very choice in point of dress.

17. A mole on either hip, shows that the person will have many children, and that they will be healthy and possess much patience.

18. A mole on the right thigh, is an indication of riches, and much happiness in the married state.

19. A mole on the left thigh, denotes poverty and want of friends through the enmity and injustice of others.

20. A mole on the right knee, shows the person will be fortunate In the choice of a partner for life, and meet with few disappointments in the world.

21. A mole on the left knee, portends that the person will be rash, inconsiderate, and hasty, but modest when in cool blood.

22. A mole on either leg, shows that the person is indolent, thoughtless, and indifferent as to whatever may happen.

23. A mole on either ankle, denotes a man to be inclined to effeminacy and elegance of dress; a lady to be courageous, active and industrious, with a trifle of the termagant.

24. A mole on either foot, forebodes sudden illness or unexpected misfortune.

25. A mole on the right shoulder, indicates prudence, discretion, secrecy, and wisdom.

26. A mole on the left shoulder, declares a testy, contentious, and ungovernable spirit.

27. A mole on the right arm, denotes vigor and courage.

28. A mole on the left arm, declares resolution and victory in battle.

Gypsy Witch Book of Old Pennsylvania Dutch Pow-Wows and Hexes

29. A mole near either elbow, denotes restlessness, a roving and unsteady temper, also a discontentedness with those which they are obliged to live constantly with.

30. A mole between the elbow and the wrist, promises the person prosperity, but not until he has undergone many hardships.

31. A mole on the wrist, or between it, and the ends of the fingers, shows industry, parsimony, and conjugal affection.

32. A mole on any part, from the shoulders to the loins, is indicative of imperceptible decline and gradual decay, whether of health or wealth.

LIST OF UNLUCKY DAYS, WHICH, TO FEMALES BORN ON THEM, WILL GENERALLY PROVE UNFORTUNATE

January 6, 6, 13, 14, 20, and 21.
February 2, 3, 9, 10, 16, 17, 22, and 23.
March 1, 2, 8, 9, 16, 17, 28, and 29.
April 24 and 25,
May 1, 2, 9, 17, 22, 29, and 30.
June 5, 6, 12, 13, 18, and 19
July 3 and 4.
September 9 and 16.
October 20 and 27.
November 9, 10, 21, 29, and 30
December 6, 14, and 21.

I, King Zoltan, particularly advise all females born on these days to be extremely cautious of placing their affections too hastily, as they will be subject to disappointments and vexations in that respect; it will be better for them (in those matters) to be guided by the advice of their friends, rather than by their own feelings, they will be less fortunate in placing their affections, than in any other action of their lives, as many of these marriages will terminate in separations, divorces, etc. Their courtships will end in elopements, seductions, and other ways not necessary of explanation.

Gypsy Witch Book of Old Pennsylvania Dutch Pow-Wows and Hexes

My readers must be well aware that affairs of importance begun at inauspicious times, by those who have been born at those periods when the stars shed their malign influence, can seldom, if ever, lead to much good: it is, therefore, that I endeavor to lay before them a correct statement drawn from accurate astrological information, in order that by strict attention and care, they may avoid falling into those perplexing labyrinths from which nothing but that care and attention can save them.

The list of days I have above given will be productive of hasty and clandestine marriages – marriages under untoward circumstances, perplexing attachments, and, as a natural consequence, the displeasure of friends, together with family dissensions, and division.

LIST OF DAYS USUALLY CONSIDERED FORTUNATE

With respect to Courtship, Marriage and Love affairs in general - females that were born on the following days may expect Court ships and prospects of Marriage which will have a happy termination.

> January 1, 2, 15, 26, 27, 28.
> February 11, 21, 26, 26.
> March 10, 24.
> April 6, 15, 16, 20, 28.
> May 3, 13, 18, 31.
> June 10, 11, 15, 22, 25.
> July 9, 14, 15, 28.
> August 6, 7, 10, 11, 16, 20, 25.
> September 4, 8, 9, 17, 18, 23.
> October 3, 7, 16, 21, 22.
> November 5, 14, 20.
> December 14, 15, 19, 20, 22, 23, 25.

Although the greater number, or indeed nearly all the ladies that are born on the days stated in the preceding list, will be likely to meet with a prospect of marriage, or become engaged in some love affair of more than ordinary importance, yet it must not be expected that the result will be the same with all of them; with some they will terminate in marriage with others in disappointment and some of them will be in danger of forming attachments that may prove of a somewhat troublesome description.

I shall, therefore, in order to enable my readers to distinguish them, give a comprehensive and useful list, showing which of them will be most likely to marry. Those born within the limits of the succeeding List of Hours, on any of the preceding days, will be the most likely to marry or win, at least, have Courtships that will be likely to have a happy termination.

THE MOON
JUDGMENTS DRAWN FROM THE MOON'S AGE

1. A child born within twenty-four hours after the new moon will be fortunate and live to a good old ace. Whatever is dreamt on that day will be fortunate and pleasing to the dreamer.

2. The second day is very lucky for discovering things lost, or hidden treasure; the child born on this day shall thrive.

3. The child born on the third day will be fortunate through persons in power, and whatever is dreamed will prove true.

4. The fourth day is bad; persons falling sick on this day rarely recover.

5. The fifth day is favorable to begin a good work, and the dreams will be tolerably successful; the child born on this day will be vain and deceitful.

6. The sixth day the dreams will not immediately come to pass and the child born will not live long.

7. On the seventh day do not tell your dreams, for much depends on concealing them; if sickness befalls you on this day, you will soon recover; the child born will livelong, but have many troubles.

Gypsy Witch Book of Old Pennsylvania Dutch Pow-Wows and Hexes

8. On the eighth day the dreams will come to pass; whatever business a person undertakes on this day will prosper.

9. The ninth day differs very little from the former; the child born on this day will arrive at great riches and honor.

10. The tenth day is likely to be fatal; those who fall sick will rarely recover, but the 2bild born on this day will live long and be a great traveler.

11. The child that is born on the eleventh day will be much devoted to religion and have an engaging form and manners.

12. On the twelfth day the dreams are rather fortunate, and the child burn shall live long.

13. On the thirteenth day the dreams will prove true in a very short time.

14. If you ask a favor of any one on the fourteenth day, it will be granted.

15. The sickness that befalls a person on the fifteenth day is likely to prove mortal.

16. The child that is born on the sixteenth day will be of very ill-manners and unfortunate; it is nevertheless a good day for the buying and selling of all kinds of merchandise.

17. The child born on the seventeenth day will be very foolish; it is a very unfortunate day to transact any kind of business, or contract marriage.

18. The child born on the eighteenth day will be vigilant, but will suffer considerable hardships; if a female, she will be chaste and industrious, and live respected to n great age.

19. The nineteenth day is dangerous; the child born will be very ill-

disposed and malicious.

20. On the twentieth day the dreams are true, but the child born will be dishonest.

21. The child born on the twenty-first day will grow up healthy and strong, but be of a very selfish, ungenteel turn of mind.

22. The child born on the twenty-second day will be fortunate; he or she will be of a cheerful countenance, religious, and much be loved.

23. The child that is born on the twenty-third day will be of an ungovernable temper, will forsake his friends, and choose to wander about in a foreign country, and will be very unhappy through life.

24. The child born on the twenty-fourth day will achieve many heroic actions, and will be much admired for his extraordinary abilities.

25. The child born on the twenty-fifth day will be very wicked; he will meet with many dangers, and is likely to come to an ill end.

26. On the twenty-sixth day the dreams are certain - the child then born will be rich, and much esteemed.

27. The twenty-seventh day is very favorable for dreams, and the child then born will be of a sweet and humble disposition.

28. The child born the twenty-eighth day will be the delight of his parents, but will not live to any great age.

29. Children born on the twenty-ninth day will experience many hardships, though in the end they may turn out happily. It is good to marry on this day; and business begun on this day will be prosperous.

30. The child that is born on the thirtieth day will be fortunate and happy, and well skilled in the arts and sciences.

Gypsy Witch Book of Old Pennsylvania Dutch Pow-Wows and Hexes

TO CAST YOUR NATIVITY

Having ascertained the exact time of your birth, and the hour in which you entered this transitory life, procure a Moore's almanac of that year, which will direct you to the sign that then reigned, the name of the planets, and the state of the moon; particularly observe whether the sun was just entering the sign, whether it was near the end, or what was its particular progress; if at the beginning, your fate will be strongly tinctured with its properties, moderate at the meridian, and slightly if the sun is nearly going out of the Write down the day of the week; see whether it is a lucky day or not, the state of the moon, the nature of the planets, and the influence described next, and you will ascertain your future destiny with very little trouble.

JANUARY
(Aquarius or the Water Bearer.)
Gives a love of wandering and variety, seldom contented long in one place; soon affronted, and slow to forgive; fond of law, though they lose the day. They are unhappy. Mercury gives them slights in love. A full moon is the best, for a new moon only adds to their false fears; and Saturn gives them real trouble to content with.

FEBRUARY
(Pisces, or the Fishes.)
Those born under the influence of this planet prosper beat on the ocean, or at a distance from their native home. But those born under this sign, and not ordained to travel, will experience at times more or less distress. Mars and Jupiter are the best planets, and if the day of the week on which they, were born be a fortunate one, let them begin their fresh concerns on that day, write and answer letters, or seek for money due to them according to their rule, and they have more than a chance for prosperity. The female traveler will be very fortunate, and have a contempt for danger, yet neither her disposition nor manners will be masculine; she will make an excellent wife and mother, and, if left a widow with children, will strive for their interest with a father's care and prudence; nor will she wed a second time, unless Venus rules her destiny, liars give her success; Jupiter, vigilance; a new moon, virtue; a full moon, some enemies; and Saturn, temptation; yet she will prosper.

Gypsy Witch Book of Old Pennsylvania Dutch Pow-Wows and Hexes

MARCH
(Aries, or the Ram.)
A very good sign to those born under it To either sex denotes prosperity, fidelity, dutiful children, and many liberal friends, but hot-tempered; if Mercury Is one of the planets, they will then be very amiable. Jupiter and Venus are also good planets to them, but Mars or Saturn causes a sad alteration to their general destiny, and gives a mixed life of wine and pleasure. Venus reigning alone as a morning star at the time of their birth causes them many amours.

APRIL
(Taurus, or the Bull.)
To be prosperous under this sign will require active industry and patience under misfortunes and perils; but Jupiter, Venus, or the new moon, will soften this destiny. The men will be bold and adventurous, fond of governing, and hard to please; they must be careful not to enter on any fresh concern while their sign has the ascendancy, the end of April and the tw6 first weeks in May.

MAY
(Gemini, or the Twins) Very fortunate for females, particularly in the grand article of matrimony, though they will prosper well in other affairs; the full moon and Venus are good for them. They will be punctual and honest in their dealings, be much respected by their friends and neighbors, and have many children.

JUNE
(Cancer, or the Crab)
A prosperous but eventful sign to both sexes, but more particularly those of a fair complexion; they will be exalted in life; Jupiter and Venus are the best signs for them; but the brunettes, though fortunate, will plague themselves and others with whims, curiosities, and ill-nature, and may be particular about mere trifles. If Man be their planet, they will enter into lawsuits; and if Saturn; let them beware of ungovernable passions.

JULY
(Leo, or the Lion)

Gypsy Witch Book of Old Pennsylvania Dutch Pow-Wows and Hexes

Favorable to those born in poverty, but not to the rich; for this sign always shows a great change of circumstances about the meridian of our days, sooner or later, according to the sign in which you were born. If Jupiter be the planet, the person born poor will become rich by legacies, or will probably marry their master or mistress, or his or her son or daughter, according to their sex, and lead a happy life. This has often proved true.

AUGUST
(Virgo, or the Virgin)
A most important sign; the men brave, generous, candid, and honest; the females amicable and prosperous, If they do not mar their own fortune by love of flattery, to which they will be prone, or else advancement awaits them. Venus is not a good planet for them, and Saturn shows seduction; but, if neither of these three planets predominate at the time of their birth, they will marry early, have good children, and enjoy the most valuable blessings of life, and have many unexpected gains.

SEPTEMBER
(Libra, or the Balance)
A middle course of life is promised by this sign; a smooth, even, unrippled stream, free from storms or sudden changes; in fact, an enviable destiny. The persons now born will be just in their transactions, faithful in love and wedlock, and averse to litigation and law; not many children, but those healthy.

OCTOBER
(Scorpio, or the Scorpion)
To the man, promises a long, active, useful life, and an intelligent mind; prosperous and very careful of what he gains; a good husband, parent and master, and a sincere friend; a little gay in his youthful days, but not vicious. Jupiter and a full moon add to the good of his destiny; Saturn or Mercury will detract from it; Venus inclines him to the fair sex. To the woman this sign shows indolence; and, if she is well off in the world, it will not be by her own merit or industry, for she will have to thank those to whom it is her good fortune to be nearly allied; but, If she has no shining qualities that are prominent, she will be free from evil propensities, and will never bring disgrace on herself, her husband,

her family, or friends, unless Venus reigned at her birth; then I fear for her; but no other planet will affect her destiny.

NOVEMBER
(Sagittarius, or the Archer)
Gives to both sexes an amorous disposition, and if Venus or Mercury presides at their birth, they will love variety; out Jupiter and Mars are good for them; the new moon is excellent to the female, add full to the man. It is seldom that persons born in this sign marry, if the first-mentioned planets reign; or, if they do marry, it is late in life, or when the meridian of their days are over, and they are become wise enough to relinquish folly; they then become steady and prudent, and generally do well; they seldom have many children, but what they have will prosper, and have friends who will promote their interest.

DECEMBER
(Capricorn, or the Goat)
Shows you will work and toil, and others reap the benefit of your labor, unless marriage) alters the destiny; out hard will be your fate if your spouse is of the same sign as yourself; but. If Jupiter be one of the planets at your birth, the end of your days will be more prosperous than the beginning, after experiencing many cares and obstructions. A woman may probably better her fate by a second marriage, especially if Venus be her planet.

LOVE PRESENTS AND WITCHING SPELLS

Take three hairs from your head, roll them up in a small compact form, and anoint them with three drops of blood from the left-hand fourth finger, choosing tills because the anatomists say a vein goes from that finger to the heart; wear this In your bosom (taking care that none knows the secret) for nine days and nights; then enclose the hair in the secret cavity of a ring or a brooch, and present it to your lover. While it is in his possession, it will have the effect of preserving his love, and leading his mind to dwell on you.

A chain or plait of your own hair, mixed with that of a goat, and anointed with nine drops of the essence of ambergris, will have a similar effect.

Flowers prepared with your own blood will have an effect on your lover's mind; but the impression will be very transient, and fade with the flowers. If your love should be fortunate, and you are married to the object of your wishes, never reveal to him the nature of the present you made him, or it may have the fatal effect of turning love into hate.

HOLY INCANTATIONS FROM THE BIBLE

CURE FOR THE COLIC

Take one fresh chicken egg and turn the small end three times in the navel of the sick baby. Say this Bible verse out loud over the baby:

Behold, if a river overflow, he trembleth not; He is confident, though a Jordan swell even to his mouth.
Job 40:23

Then bury the egg on the North end of the house.

The mother of the baby should then burn a white onion in hog lard and remove the burnt pieces. Mash this up to make a salve and rub this on the baby's stomach morning and night for nine days. On the ninth day the baby will stop crying.

STOP PAIN

Find a smooth creek stone big enough to fit into the palm of your hand. Hold the stone on the forehead of the one who is in pain and say the following chant:

*Hair and hide, Flesh and blood,
Nerve and bone, No more pain than this stone.*

Next say the following Bible verse:

and they lifted up their voices, saying,
Jesus, Master, have mercy on us.
Luke 17:13

TO LIFT A CURSE

If someone complains of being cursed, lay your hands on their shoulders and silently say the following:

Lord Jesus, thy wounds so red will guard me against death. Lord Jesus, thy suffering so profound will guard me against pain. Lord Jesus, thy tears so cleansing will guard me against evil.

TO RELEASE SOMEONE WHO IS SPELL-BOUND

This can be done for someone who is in your presence or at a distance. If the person is far-away, make sure no creek or river is between you. Say this out loud:

You horseman and footman, whom I here conjured at this time, you may pass on in the name of Jesus Christ, through the word of God and the will of Christ; ride ye on now and pass.

Next, read this Bible verse to yourself:

Unto the upright there ariseth light in the darkness: He is' gracious, and merciful, and righteous.
Psalms 112:4

TO BE BLESSED AT ALL TIMES

To be assured of Gods blessing everyday, say this silently to yourself in the morning upon arising from bed:

Gypsy Witch Book of Old Pennsylvania Dutch Pow-Wows and Hexes

I conjure thee, sword, sabre or knife, that mightest injure or harm me, by the priest of all prayers, who had gone into the temple at Jerusalem, and said: An edged sword shall pierce your soul that you may not injure me, who am a child of God.

TO ASSURE GOD'S BLESSING TO A LOVED ONE

If there is someone you love and want them to receive God's blessing and protection, without telling them what you are doing, say their name out loud when the sun rises in the morning and then say silently:

Like unto the cup and the wine, and the holy supper, which our dear Lord Jesus Christ gave unto his dear disciples on Maunday Thursday, may the Lord Jesus guard [name] in daytime, and at night, that no dog may bite [name], no wild beast tear [name] to pieces, no tree fall on [name], no water rise against [name], no fire-arms injure [name], no weapons, no steel, no iron, cut [name], no fire burn [name], no false sentence fall upon [name], no false tongue injure [name], no rogue enrage [name], and that no fiends, no witchcraft and enchantment can harm [name]. Amen.

TO SPELL-BIND ANYTHING

Say the Lord's Prayer three times, then say:

Christ's cross and Christ's crown, Christ Jesus' colored blood, be thou every hour good. God, the Father, is before me; God, the Son, is beside me; God, the Holy Ghost, is behind me. Whoever now is stronger than these three persons may come, by day or night, to attack me.

A CURE FOR WOUNDS

Take the bones of a calf, and burn them until they turn to powder, and then strew it into the wound. Next, recite this Bible verse:

Gypsy Witch Book of Old Pennsylvania Dutch Pow-Wows and Hexes

Receive him therefore in the Lord with all joy; and hold such in honor: because for the work of Christ he came nigh unto death, hazarding his life to supply that which was lacking in your service toward me.
Philippians 2:29-30

The powder prevents the flesh from putrefying, and is therefore of great importance in healing the wound.

Another cure is for cuts and scratches on a child. Place both of your hands on the head of a hurt child and say:

Mother Mary stop thy crying, Mother Mary stop thy pain. With your son's blood speak truth from these lips.

A REMEDY FOR BURNS

To relieve the pain and heal a burn, say this Bible verse to yourself:
Now the God of hope fill you with all joy and peace in believing, that ye may abound in hope, in the power of the Holy Spirit. Romans 15:13

Next, say this out loud:

Clear out, brand, but never in; be thou cold or hot, thou must cease to burn. May God guard thy blood and thy flesh, thy marrow and thy bones, and every artery, great or small. They all shall be guarded and protected in the name of God against inflammation and mortification, in the name of God the Father, the Son, and the Holy Ghost. Amen.

This can be done in the presence of those that are injured, or to heal someone from a distance.

A WAY TO FIND LOVE FOR THOSE WHO SEEK

Take a piece of red ribbon and wrap it three times around the wrist of those seeking love. With each wrap, say these words:

Gypsy Witch Book of Old Pennsylvania Dutch Pow-Wows and Hexes

Oh Song of Songs find thee love. Oh Song of Songs bring thee love. Oh Song of Songs keep thee love.

Wear the ribbon for three days and at the end of the third day, remove the ribbon and place it in a Bible to insure God's blessing.

KEEP POVERTY AT BAY

To keep poverty from taking everything away from you or a friend, take a length of black thread from an unused spool. Starting from the bottom, tie seven knots throughout the length of the thread and recite out loud with each knot:

For we are God's workmanship, created in Christ Jesus to do good works, which God prepared in advance for us to do.
Ephesians 2:10

Place the thread in a small bag and whoever needs it, carry it with him at all times to keep poverty away.

FOR A DIFFICULT PREGNANCY

If a woman is worried that the baby she is carrying will be premature or breach, take a bowl of fresh rainwater and dip your finger in it. With your wet finger, make the sign of the cross on the stomach of the pregnant woman and say out loud:

May it please thee O, Eel Chad, to grant unto this woman [name] daughter of [name], that she may not at this time, or at any other time, have a premature confinement; much more grant unto her a truly fortunate delivery, and keep her and the fruit of the body in good health.

If a woman is having trouble conceiving, say this: *Lord and Lady. Mother and Father. Life Divine. Gift [name] with a healthy child.*

Gypsy Witch Book of Old Pennsylvania Dutch Pow-Wows and Hexes

TO HAVE GOOD FORTUNE

This is for anyone who has been unlucky despite their best efforts. Say this Bible verse three times before the sun rises:

And they that are wise shall shine as the brightness of the firmament; and they that turn many to righteousness as the stars for ever and ever.
Daniel 12:3

TO OVERCOME WICKED PEOPLE

To stop anyone who means to do you or your loved ones harm, say the following Bible verse:

One of themselves, a prophet of their own, said, Cretans are always liars, evil beasts, idle gluttons.
Titus 1:12

PROTECT YOUR HOME AND BELONGINGS

Write the following sacred names on a clean piece of white paper:

SATOR, AREPO, TENET, OPERA, ROTAS.

Seal them in a small bag that can be tied or sewn shut. Place the bag near your front door.

CURE FOR THE HEADACHE

Tame thou flesh and bone, like Christ in Paradise; and who will assist thee, this I tell thee [name] for your repentance sake.

This you must say three times, each time lasting for three minutes, and your headache will soon cease.

Gypsy Witch Book of Old Pennsylvania Dutch Pow-Wows and Hexes

TO LIVE HAPPY AND BE PROSPEROUS

Say this verse once a day, every day:

Thou wilt shew me the path of life; in thy presence is fullness of joy; at thy right hand there are pleasures for evermore.
Psalms 16:11

DREAMS
How to Receive Oracles by Dreams

He who would receive true dreams, should keep a pure, undisturbed, and imaginative spirit, and so compose it that it may be made worthy of knowledge and government by the mind; for such a spirit is most fit for prophesying, and is a most clear glass of all images which flow everywhere from all things. When, therefore, we are sound in body, not disturbed in mind, our intellect not made dull by heavy meats and strong drink, not sad through poverty, not provoked through lust, not incited by any vice, nor stirred up by wrath or anger, not being irreligiously and profanely inclined, not given to levity nor lost to drunkenness, but, chastely going to bed, fall asleep, then our pure and divine soul being free from all the evils above recited, and separated from all hurtful thoughts-and now freed, by dreaming is endowed with this divine spirit as an instrument, and doth receive those beams and representations which are darted down, as it were, and shine forth from, the divine Hind into itself, in a deifying glass.

There are four kinds of true dreams, viz., the first, matutine, i.e., between sleeping and waking; the second, that which one sees concerning another; the third, that whose interpretation is shown to the same dreamer in the nocturnal vision; and, lastly, that which-is related to the same dreamer in the nocturnal vision. But natural things and their own co-mixtures do likewise belong unto wise men, and we often use such to receive oracles from a spirit by a dream, which are either by perfumes, unctions, meats, drinks, rings, seals, etc.

Gypsy Witch Book of Old Pennsylvania Dutch Pow-Wows and Hexes

Now those who are desirous to receive oracles through a dream, let them make themselves a ring of the Sun or Saturn for this purpose. There are likewise images of dreams, which, being put under the head when going to sleep, doth effectually give true dreams of whatever the mind hath before determined or consulted upon, the practice of which is as follows:

Thou Shalt make an image of the Sun, the figure whereof must be a man sleeping upon the bosom of an angel; which thou shall make when Leo ascends, the Sun being in the ninth house in Aries; then you must write upon the figure the name of the effect desired, and in the hand of the angel the name and character of the intelligence of the Sun, which is Michael.

Let the same Image be made in Virgo ascending--Mercury being fortunate in Aries in the ninth, or Gemini ascending, Mercury being fortunate in the ninth house in Aquarius and let him be received by Saturn with a fortunate aspect, and let the name of the spirit (which is Raphael) be written upon it. Let the same likewise be made-Libra ascending, Venus being received from Mercury in Gemini in the ninth house-and write upon it the name of the angel of Venus (which is Anacl). Again you may make the same image-Aquarius ascending, Saturn fortunately possessing the ninth in his exaltation, which is Libra-and let there be written upon it the name of the angel of Saturn (which is Cassial). The same may be made with Cancer ascending, the Moon being received by Jupiter and Venus in Pisces, and being fortunately placed in the ninth house-and write upon it the spirit of the Moon (which is Gabriel).

There are likewise made rings of dreams of wonderful efficacy, and there are rings of the Sun and Saturn-and the constellation of them in, when the Sun or Saturn ascend in their exaltation in the ninth, and when the Moon is joined to Saturn in the ninth, and in that sign which was the ninth house of the nativity, and write and engrave upon the rings the name of the spirit of the Sun or Saturn; and by these rules you may know how and by what means to constitute more of yourself. But know this, that such images work nothing (as they are simply images), except they are vivified by spiritual and celestial virtue, and chiefly by the ardent desire and firm intent of the soul of the operator. But who can give a soul to an image, or make a stone, or metal, or clay, or wood, or wax, or paper, to live? Certainly no man whatever; for this arcanum doth not enter into an artist of a stiff neck. He only hath it who transcends the progress of angels, and comes to the very Archtype Himself. The tables of numbers likewise confer to the receiving of oracles, being duly formed under their own constellations.

Therefore, he who is desirous of receiving true oracles by dreams, let him abstain from supper, from drink, and be otherwise well disposed, so his brain will be free from turbulent vapors; let him also have his bedchamber fair and clean, exorcised and consecrated; then let him perfume the same with some convenient fumigation, and let him anoint his temples with some unguent efficacious hereunto, and put a ring of dreams upon his finger; then let him take one of the images we have spoken of, and place the same under his head; then let him address himself to sleep, meditating upon that thing which he desires to know. So shall he receive a most certain and undoubted oracle by a dream when the Moon goes through the sign of the ninth revolution of his nativity, and when she is in the ninth sign from the sign of perfection.

This is the way whereby we may obtain all sciences and arts whatsoever, whether astrology, occult philosophy, physic, etc. or else suddenly and perfectly with a true Illumination of our Intellect, although all inferior familiar spirits whatsoever conduce to this effect, and sometimes also evil spirits sensibly inform us, intrinsically and extrinsically.

FINGER-NAIL OBSERVATIONS

Broad nails show the person to be bashful, fearful, but of gentle nature.

When there is a certain white mark at the extremity of them, it shows that the person has more honesty than subtlety, and that his worldly substance will be impaired through negligence.
Long white nails denote much sickness and infirmity, especially fevers, an indication of strength and deceit by women. If upon the white

anything appears at the extremity that is pale, it denotes short life by sudden death, and the person to be given to melancholy.

When there appears a certain mixed redness, of colors, at the beginning of the nails, it shows the person to be choleric and quarrelsome.

When the extremity is black it is a sign of husbandry.

Narrow nails denote the person to be inclined to mischief and to do injury to his neighbor.

Long nails show the person to be good-natured, but mistrustful, and loves reconciliation rather than differences.

Oblique nails signify deceit and want of courage, little and round nails denote obstinate anger and hatred. If they be crooked at the extremity, they show pride and fierceness.

Round nails show a choleric person, yet soon reconciled, honest, and a lover of secret sciences.

Fleshy nails denote the person to be mild in his temper, idle, and lazy pale and black nails show the person to he very deceitful to his neighbor, and subject to many diseases.

Red and marked nails signify a choleric and martial nature, given to cruelty; and, as many little marks aft there are, they speak of so many evil desires.

TRADITIONAL WAY TO BAFFLE YOUR ENEMIES

Repeat reverently, and with sincere faith, the following words, and you will be protected in the hour of danger:

"Behold, God is my salvation; I will trust, and not be afraid, for the Lord Jehovah is my strength and my song; he also is become my salvation.
"For the stars of heaven, and the constellation thereof, shall not give

their light; the sun shall be darkened in his going forth, and the moon shall not cause her tight to shine.

"And behold, at eventide, trouble; and before morning he is not; this is the portion of them that spoil us, and the lot of them that rob us."

CHARM AGAINST TROUBLE IN GENERAL

Repeat reverently, and with sincere faith, the following words, and you shall be protected in the hour of danger:

"He shall deliver thee in six troubles, yea, in seven there shall no evil touch thee; in famine he shall redeem thee from death, and in war from the power of the sword; and thou shall know that thy tabernacle shall be in peace, and thou shalt visit thy habitation and shall not err."

Gypsy Witch Book of Old Pennsylvania Dutch Pow-Wows and Hexes

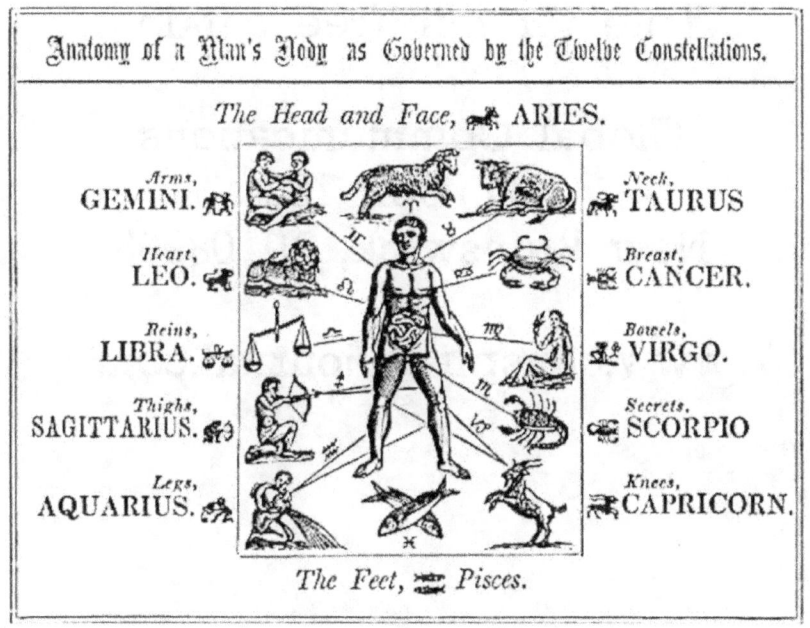

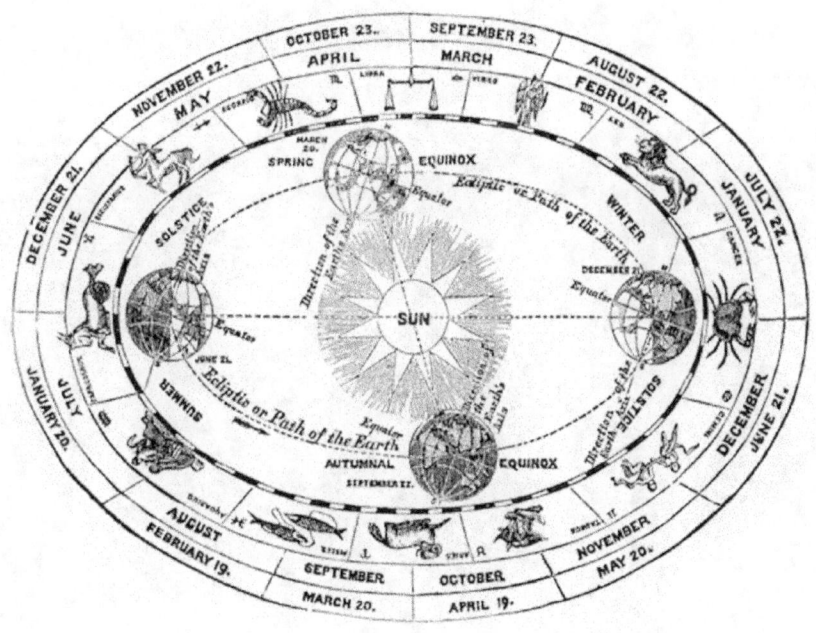

Write for our free catalog:

Global Communications
P.O. Box 753
New Brunswick, NJ 08903

www.conspiracyjournal.com